FREE
HAPPINESS

TESTIMONIALS

"This book creates such a strong personal connection that is hard to elicit when dealing with factual topics. I read a lot of business, personal development books and in general they don't resonate in the same way. So many powerful techniques and suggestions are wrapped up here in both anecdote and science; a terrific balance."

– Clive Betts, Head of People Development, University of Exeter

"Free Happiness gives you the best of both worlds – insights from a respected clinical psychologist in the field of happiness, as well as personal stories that reveal her lived experiences, reminding us we're not alone on this journey. Be prepared to see happiness, yourself and the world differently. But most importantly, prepare to be inspired."

– Eric Moeller, Director of Product Marketing, Sage

"How refreshing to read such an informative and entertaining work from an author so highly qualified in this relatively new field of the science of happiness. I have a better understanding of how we can become happier people and have a glowing feeling of, 'Yes, I see that now'. I find myself wanting to know more about her captivating life experiences."

– Vik's Dad, Chief Optimism Officer

"Thank you for this beautiful girl, who looks after everybody. We've all got to play our part in protecting the world, we need to work as one."

– Sir Richard Branson, Entrepreneur, Necker Island

FREE HAPPINESS

The art and science of positivity

DR VIKKI BARNES

ISBN: 979-8-5265-4659-1

To Mum and Dad, for helping to create my world.

CONTENTS

CONTENTS

Part Three: Emotions for life

Part Four: Enabling greatness

ABOUT THE AUTHOR

Vikki is a humanitarian, nature lover and adventurer, deeply passionate about people and the planet – a true believer in change for good. Uniquely, she is a clinical psychologist working with a wide range of private, public and corporate industries as their organisational consultant for happiness and wellbeing. She's an expert in positive psychology and feeds inspiration to the world as an international speaker. She's originally from a rural village in North Staffordshire, England.

In 2011, Vikki qualified with a doctorate in clinical and community psychology at the University of Exeter, having previously completed a master's degree in cognitive neuropsychology at Oxford Brookes University and a bachelor's degree in psychology and applied social studies at Keele University. During her second undergraduate year, she studied at the University of Texas.

With over 10 years of NHS service, Vikki provided mental health interventions and education to patients and staff. For several years she worked with Virgin, where she designed and led their national wellbeing programme, working alongside leaders and executives, embedding effective practices into the company ethos.

In 2018, Vikki was asked to work in the British Virgin

Islands with Sir Richard Branson, to set up mental health provision for survivors following hurricane Irma. She worked with the community and health professionals, developing support services.

In 2019, Vikki founded Positive Wellbeing, which is an organisational wellbeing consultancy offering proactive, preventive mental health consultation, programmes, coaching, inspirational talks and award-winning retreats across the globe. Her client list includes universities, schools, healthcare, the armed forces, aviation, seafarers, law firms, management companies, property agents. Championing the Wellbeing Economy, Vikki promotes positive leadership and a movement towards a better world.

Vikki says, "I've always been fascinated by people. I love travelling and meeting people around the world, learning about their culture, environments and experiences. I'm always seeking new ways that we can look after ourselves and our planet, whilst having fun in the process.

My aim is to be real and I enjoy helping others to feel good. I've got things wrong, I've had some dark moments, I've felt regret and shame. I have vulnerabilities and scars that I've struggled with and still struggle with. I'm optimistic, relentlessly hopeful, believe in the good of humanity and making the world a better place. I see great value in connection, authenticity, gratitude, vulnerability and compassion. Difficult times and living a good life can go hand in hand if we accept it all as part of our agreement with life and be truly, wildly and wonderfully ourselves.

The idea of this book was born when I attended an international conference as a keynote speaker in the Netherlands. I had my talk all planned out; I was ready to address topics I was used to presenting to large groups – mental health and wellbeing, grounded in the science of positive psychology. Right before the conference I changed my mind. I love my work and would have gladly spoken about just that, but I had an overwhelming urge to bring something new this time. Something that I was deeply passionate about, something I had no idea would land well or make sense, but somehow I just had to go for it. I realised this was my intuition and I listened to it. It's that sense of feeling that you just "can't not" do something, no matter how little it fits with your plan, or what others expect of you. I'm glad I followed my instinct because I talked about the topics that now make up the following chapters. I wonder whether I was destined to write it all along. I know, psychologists are known for delving into the past to find links from our earlier lives to our later behaviours. I won't analyse that; to be honest I'm not your "average" psychologist in that sense, because I prefer to focus forwards, but the desire to share these ideas has been within me for a very long time, perhaps forever. This is my favoured approach to change – spending time and energy cultivating the life we desire, rather than ruminating on the hard times or the mistakes we've made. Let's set about making some worthwhile and positive changes in our lives. We all have the power to do that. It begins with knowing yourself and how you want to be.

I've always been somewhat of an enigma. My paternal grandmother saw the daydreamer in me and my maternal grandmother saw the brain scientist! I'm half professional, suiting up with my briefcase to inspire great minds around the world, and half nomad, driving into the wilderness with my beloved camper van with no plan other than to be out there a while. My dad taught me practical tips because I like understanding how things work, and my mum encouraged a dreamland because I'm a fan of romance. My world is definitely not simple, it's brilliantly complex, a joy to me. We all have a choice. The choice to create the world in which we want to live. That's what this is all about.

When I was a little girl I wanted to do three things: go on lots of adventures, make my parents proud and help other people feel good. I've travelled extensively in my years on this earth so far, to several continents and many countries, racking up those experiences and taking in diverse cultures, making friends all over the globe and learning a lot about myself. I loved every moment, even though some of it was tough, lonely and downright frightening at times. I've been on some fantastic journeys through my personal and work life, which I dreamed of doing for as long as I can remember. When I was a child, conjuring up these adventures in my mind, I even had a theme tune, as every good explorer would. I went on so many expeditions and my imagination was my only limit. In my adult life, I made a lot of these adventures a reality, though I didn't realise it at the time; it's only when I began writing this book and reflecting back that I saw myself living out the dreams of that young girl. My parents tell me I've made them proud, which is lovely to hear for someone who values that. I remember their teary yet smiley eyes on my graduation days, especially when I became a doctor. I feel we ought to appreciate our elders more and I hope they know how grateful I am for the start they gave to me. Making them proud is my way of extending that gratitude. My third ambition was to help people feel good, so it's no surprise that I should choose a career in clinical psychology and perhaps even less of a surprise for me to find myself drawn to a specialism of positive psychology and happiness. Maybe I've already achieved the ambitions I had for myself, although I know there are more, which I'm yet to discover and hope with all my heart that I get there.

We were all youthful once, with big dreams and plans that we hoped we'd make a reality. Did you make it? If we'd had the cognitive capacity at a young age to consider what's really important in life, we'd have put our own happiness high on that personal agenda from day one. I'm not saying it's always easy but it is worth it. We have a lifetime to achieve our aspirations, and we simply don't know how long that is for each of us. So let's get to it, shall we?

My desire? To make a positive difference in the world of mental wellbeing, inspiring people that the best thing they can be is authentic.

My hope? That you'll take away new learnings and realisations that will help change your life in a good way.

My dream? To live in a world where we value human and

environmental connection above all else, where people connect with other people and with this wonderful planet as one big fantastic and unbelievable occurrence!

My expectation? That at least two people (the proud parents) will buy my book and I'll have a gargantuan sense of achievement that I put some of my most important messages out there into the world, which if nothing else, has been yet another adventure."

THE BEGINNING

Beginnings and endings are so important.

First impressions, lasting impressions.

The first time. The last time.

Moving in. Moving out.

Arriving. Leaving.

Our first moments on Earth. Our final moments on Earth.

Because of the orbiting of our planet around the Sun and the rotation on its own axis, we have one beginning and one ending every single day. As the average human being lives for approximately 80 years, that gives us 58,400 chances to create the best beginnings and endings in our lifetime. If our lifetime is shorter than that, then this means those opportunities are even more precious. We can create great beginnings and endings every day. Yesterday I began with yoga in the park and ended with a moonlight sea swim. Did it impact upon my day, my mood and my mental wellbeing? Absolutely! And that's only one example; we have plenty of beginnings and endings that happen elsewhere in our lives too. They are all opportunities and we can make them count, make them memorable and make them a part of our happiness history.

To get the most out of this book, start as you mean to go on. Take action as you go. When we learn something new and interesting, we often feel inspired to build these learnings into our lives, then we get distracted and lose momentum. I want this to make a difference for you and a good one at that! I suggest getting yourself a journal or notepad to scribble the bits that resonate. Better still, scribble on the pages – go on, life's for living! Read one chapter at a time, then put the book down for a few days whilst you figure out how to bring one thing from that chapter into your life, for the better. Embed it into your daily routine, whether it be changing the way you think or creating a new behavioural habit. Move through the chapters in this way, one by one and by the time you've finished, you'll have improved your life in many ways, reaping the rewards of feeling great! Your scribbles are your reminders of what matters to you; they are important because we don't always get it right the first time around and most of us forget what we've learned unless we keep it fresh. Make your changes meaningful and sustainable.

For those of you who wouldn't dream of scribbling in a book, I've lifted some ideas from each chapter and included brief notes at the end, as a starting point for your positive wellbeing toolkit. Dip into them as you go, or leave them until you've finished. They are suggestions for action and yours for the taking.

Welcome to the beginning. Make it count. Find a cosy spot to sit and relax whilst you read. Make your favourite drink to enjoy at the same time. Open your mind and your heart. Remove distractions. Smile and enjoy.

PART ONE: FREE YOURSELF

HEALTH IS MENTAL

It's for all of us

Some people think that mental health is not for them. A topic they are uninterested in or don't need to worry about. Or a topic they just don't have time to properly consider. They may think mental difficulties won't touch them, because of their carefree nature or the way they see the world, letting negativity blissfully pass by. I see mental health as something that is for everyone. It is unpredictable and nobody is immune to a little (or large) mental health blip. Liken it to when you were a teenager and your parents told you they understood what you were going through, because they'd been there once and had experienced similar things. Or when they told you how you'd see the world differently someday, when you matured a little. You may have retaliated or thought, "No way, I'm different and am never going to think or behave the way my parents do!" Before you know it, you're in a garden centre getting excited about the plethora of veg on offer to grow back home! It's an analogy for mental health difficulties, in that, if you've been through it then you understand it's out there and something that can happen to anyone, anytime. Whereas if you haven't experienced it then it remains somewhat mystical, as though external and not a part of your life. Until, of course, it is. That's the time we reflect and think, "Ah, perhaps I should've heard the advice and put something in place to be more prepared and ready for this." That's what I believe my work is all about. At the very least, if you don't need it right at this moment, there will be someone close to you who does, so learning ways to support mental health in general is always a step in the right direction.

The world is finally waking up to the need to look at mental health in a different way. It's a slow process but we're already making great leaps to understanding this phenomenon differently. Many research studies offer a head-spinning number of statistics about who experiences what mental difficulties and when; psychologists spend countless hours working out why it happens and what on earth to do with it. The general consensus is that mental health problems affect 1 in 4 of us. This is our first myth. That figure is actually 1 in 1. None of us are devoid of mental health, just as none of us are devoid of physical health. We all experience peaks and dips in our physical fitness and we go through the ups and downs of mental fitness in the same way. We all have mental and physical wellbeing, the difference is how society has trained us to see them so differently.

The mental health spectrum

This is our first challenge – to view mental health as something we all have, to understand mental health as a great thing (it's health, after all!) and to accept that none of us are immune to difficulties in our mental health from time to time. Of course, mental ill health is a spectrum and just as with any good spectrum, there are extremes. These extremes may require a clinician's input, a diagnosis, treatment even. For the most part however, each and every one of us can take steps to improving our mental health on a day to day basis and the first step is to remove the lens we've been looking at this phenomenon through all these years and see it differently. We are all together on this. As certain as we were born and someday we will die, we will all have good days and bad days when it comes to how emotionally or psychologically well we're feeling.

To manage expectations early on in your reading, I must confess that I'm not a huge fan of statistics and prescriptive models. Partly because my brain doesn't seem to work naturally in that detailed way and it was my most distressing module as I fumbled my way through my doctoral qualification, but mostly because constrained approaches can lead us to make assumptions when it would be more helpful for us to remain more open minded. To use a crude but humorous example: the average human has one testicle. Think about that for a moment. It's statistically viable, but not quite right somehow. Having said that, allow me to return to a couple of figures for the purpose of illustration. Statistics can work incredibly well when their mere poignancy makes you stop and think and hopefully make some changes in your life. For every 20 people who call in sick to work because of their mental health, only 1 feels able to tell the truth. 19 out of 20 people make up a physical ailment because it is deemed more acceptable. There is 1 suicide every 2 hours in the UK and 1 suicide every 40 seconds in the world. The main reasons for this are stigma around mental health and people not feeling able to openly express how much they're struggling.

A global shift

We need to help change this. We need to talk about mental health, the way we talk about physical health. We need to open up, be seen, be strong in being vulnerable, show up as who we truly are and what we're going through. We need to slow down, notice, recognise suffering and help each other. We need to do this for ourselves, for those we love and for our world. We can all be part of the solution. A global culture shift begins with us and I believe that it begins with being simply and authentically human.

There are two ways we can instantly assist in the creation of a healthy mindset, no matter what we're going through. The first is radical acceptance. The second is recognising the beauty of a full spectrum of experiences and emotions as a much better way to spend a life, than the mere existence of the simple and not so satisfying "okay". I hope to take you on a journey of both as you read on.

To get us into the right mindset, award winning author and social justice activist L. R. Knost (2013) encapsulates this perfectly when she says, "Life is amazing. And then it's awful. And then it's amazing again. And in between the amazing and the awful, it's ordinary and mundane and routine. Breathe in the amazing, hold on through the awful, and relax and inhale during the ordinary. That's just living a heartbreaking, soul-healing, amazing, awful, ordinary life. And it's breathtakingly beautiful." The first time I read this, it gave me goosebumps. Because it's true.

DESIRE TO BE HAPPY

How do you find that much chased and envied "happiness" through it all? As it turns out, it's easy when you know how.

One joyous day way back, you were born. One sad day in the future, you will die. The time in between those two days are yours to do everything you'll ever do and in the manner you choose. Lots of good, bad and indifferent things will happen during that time too. You're not in control of it all but you are in control of one thing. Is this time in between those two momentous days going to be spent by you happily, or unhappily?

Happiness is limitless

How many choices do you suppose you'll make in your lifetime? What to wear, where to study, who to hang out with, where to work, who to have a relationship with, whether to have children, what political stance to take, where to live, what to have for dinner ... Which of these choices is the single most important one? It's the one that's the ultimate goal, no matter what else happens or doesn't happen. Still wondering? It's whether or not to be happy. That's it. Happiness should take the lead and everything else should follow. If you decide to live your best life, then everything that happens will flow through that lens, as long as you don't attempt to qualify that happiness with statements like "as long as I find the perfect partner" or "when I get that promotion". Feeling good isn't bound up in external factors when you make the decision to be happy no matter what. Happiness is quite simply yours, if you genuinely want it. Happiness isn't finite, it's limitless. It's out there for you and you can have as much of it as you like. Of course, when life is dancing along smoothly, this is an easy feat. When adversity surprises us, maintaining this path becomes challenging, yet remains possible. As long as you really mean it when you choose it, then it's yours, because you'll have committed to that decision and that is the ultimate human existence.

If we're in agreement that happiness is our most important decision then we can go ahead and discuss its many facets. I've gathered some of the most significant aspects of happiness that I've found to be worthwhile considering, in my many years of research, clinical and corporate work (not to mention my own life experience) and popped them into chapters here for you to peruse and ponder. I practise what I preach and all my suggestions are tried and tested by me (and many others!). Being your best isn't always easy, it's not all about being joyful on the outside, it isn't even about feeling like everything's okay all the time. It's complex, testing, rewarding and magnificent. It's about being raw and real, knowing and being yourself. To explore and enhance your best chance at wellbeing is the most worthwhile endeavour and the best way to spend your days on Earth (or wherever you choose to be).

I've spent the last 20 years dedicating my work to helping people and last 10 years researching and applying positive psychology, trying out different ways that we can all improve our mental health, no matter who we are, where we've come from or where we're going. It excites and invigorates me to talk and write about what I've found and my hope is that it inspires you to make even one small change in your own life, which will have a beneficial impact on your wellbeing.

It makes all the hours I've spent already worthwhile. Deeper than that, I'm starting to realise this is a part of my purpose and essentially why I'm here.

Positive psychology

I spent many years in public health and social care services, in private support services, in corporate organisations and working alongside groups and individuals with a wide variety of difficulties, questions, concerns and goals. Clinical psychology training taught me a range of methods to delve into the lives of those people, assess their experiences, formulate a solution, offer therapeutic intervention and evaluate our progress based on which symptoms were eradicated and which persisted. There is, of course, a place for all kinds of psychological intervention and therapy and they all work when done well. To me though, none of them felt quite right; they didn't make me feel I was working authentically. Then I came across this relatively new and exciting model: positive psychology.

In a nutshell, this is the science of happiness, the science of a life worth living. It's about proactively putting in place simple and effective techniques that are easy to pop into your daily life yet have a huge impact when done with determination. It's about focusing on what we want and cultivating more of those things. It leads us into living a good life, a meaningful life and a pleasurable life. What I love most about the model is that it changes the way we view mental health. If we consider mental health as a continuum, whereby most of us are bumbling around at zero most of the time (we're middling), when we're doing okay but not feeling great, nor unwell. Then when negative life events occur, our resilience wanes, we lean into one of those mental health dips and move down the continuum into minus figures. Traditionally, psychology aims to bring us from the negative, back to middling, because this is the absence of difficulty, it's where symptoms are reduced to an acceptable level and where most of us are used to living.

This saddens me immensely and I certainly don't wish to look back at the end of my days and know that I led a mediocre, average life of just being okay.

When travelling in Australia in my twenties, I saw this quote and I've never forgotten it: "I'd rather have lived 20 years than just been there for 80." You'll understand then, why I was so energised by positive psychology, with its ultimate aim of bringing people not only from minus to zero, but beyond the middle ground and into the plus side. The questions asked include: "What makes us happier?"

I've proposed this to thousands of people over the years and one of our most common goals, which we share as human beings, is that we have a desire and drive to be happy. This is fantastic news as it's our motivation and inspires us to change. There are a few people who don't seem to share this desire and if this is you, then we may agree to disagree. Cherophobia exists after all: a fear of happiness, an aversion to positive feelings and deliberate avoidance of pleasurable emotions. In any case, whether we strive to be happy or simply not unhappy, there is a call to make large and rapid changes to the global mental health crisis and I believe we can all do that by living our lives with more awareness of a few simple things.

What I realised when researching and developing my practices was that taking care of our mental wellbeing doesn't have to be difficult, take lots of time, or cost money. Quite the opposite in fact, it can be woven into our daily lives, it can be free and incredibly enjoyable.

From years of reflecting, pondering, questioning, challenging, reading and experiencing, I came to the conclusion that there are a set of human qualities that occur naturally within us all and can be cultivated to improve our satisfaction with life. After all, we may well only get this one, so we ought to live it well.

Let's dive in. I'd like you to open your mind to be as accepting and willing as you can. That way, I hope my musings resonate with you.

KINDNESS AND GRATITUDE

Let me start with one of the first things I realised had a profound effect on my mental health and something we can all make better use of. Gratitude.

It is, by definition, the quality of being thankful; readiness to show appreciation for and to return kindness.

Being more grateful

Think of one thing you're grateful for right now; one thing in your life that you're so glad you have. Take a moment to dive deeper into the reasons you're grateful for this and how it makes you feel. We spend significantly less time thinking about things we're grateful for than things we don't have and would like more of, or things others have that we don't.

Neuropsychological studies show us that the information we feed into our brains has a huge impact on how our brains function going forwards. Brains function like muscles, so we can strengthen the bits we like and want more of, such as good thoughts.

When we do this our worlds appear to become better and we feel more optimistic. This is because of the input we're offering to our brains. As an example, have you ever focused on the one thing that went wrong during your day, even when lots of other things went well? How about when you made a mistake or failed at something and subsequently berated yourself. Using negative language and reprimanding yourself changes the neuronal activity of your brain, by assisting it to pick up on the negatives. This, of course, affects your mental health. What we need to do is switch those negative self statements to positive ones. So a brutal post-failure internal dialogue of "I can't believe you messed that up!" becomes a kind, compassionate and infinitely more healthy "You did your best and you're still a great person!" Now we know that our brains are taking all of this in as input to decipher our worlds and respond accordingly, imagine the impact if we were to reframe all our negative statements. The advice is simple: replace the negative with positive.

Brené Brown is a Texan professor and author and one of my biggest inspirations. She believes that gratitude is the antidote to foreboding joy. I love this concept, because it's so true and makes me smile every time I realise it's happening to me or to someone else. Foreboding joy is a fearful apprehension that something bad will happen in moments of joy. We do it to ourselves, in that when we experience true happiness, we consciously replace some of those excitable emotions with warnings of all the possible tragedies that might occur as a result of being so unashamedly happy! It's where phrases such as, "Expect the worse and anything else is a bonus" or "Merry nights bring sorry mornings" come from (the latter being one of my grandmother's personal favourites). It's preparing for the worst even when things are at their best, which is a shame when the alternative is to bask in the glory of things going well (which incidentally, would also be beautifully mindful). Because of this, joy can feel vulnerable. To me, that means that joy is courageous. Gratitude in times of joy is our best route to staying blissfully in the moment. So be grateful and bask away!

Random acts of kindness

There are plenty of ways to become ever more kind and appreciative. One of my favourites is a random act of kindness. This can be anything, big or small, that brings goodness to someone else. An example might be paying a compliment, buying a gift, offering help or being there for a friend in need. A simple smile in the street could put a spring in the step of your passerby, making them more likely to pass that smile on to their next acquaintance and so the kindness continues. If you'd like to learn new gratitude practices, there are three methods I use which never fail to have a nice influence on my mood.

The first is make a gratitude statement, first thing in the morning, as soon as you wake up (and remember to do so!). Say something out loud like, "I'm so glad I woke up early enough to see the sunrise this morning." Let the good mood envelop you and smile at your skilful start to the day. The second method is to write down what you're thankful for, perhaps one to three things that you wouldn't want to be without right now. Writing them down uses different parts of your brain, which can feel like it solidifies these elements of your life even more, almost as though they become greater. That's a nifty little trick! The third way is to tell someone how grateful you are and why. Having a conversation enhances the concept of gratitude in your mind, as you need to think about ways of ensuring someone else understands, using language and complex thought processes to explore the corners of your treasured experiences. Not only that, having someone respond to your gratefulness and reflect it back at you, perhaps with a statement or a question, cements it further still. By this point your brain is awash with happy hormones and no doubt having a lovely effect on the person you're sharing with too – but more on this later.

Cultivating a brain full of kindness and gratitude is one of the single most beneficial exercises you can commit to in order to live a more pleasurable life. So go for it, make a grateful statement each morning, either to yourself or to someone else, out loud or in writing. Tell someone about it and ask them what they're thankful for too. You'll create a high moment for yourself and might even set them off on a high too. There's a random act of kindness and a very good deed in itself!

If you decide to practise gratitude before bed, be sure to focus on the good things that happened during your day, noticing what you have to be thankful for and why. There's always something, every single day, even if it seems small. Every good thing is significant.

CONNECTION

The definition of connection is a relationship in which a person or thing is linked or associated with something else. Not a particularly special description of something so wonderfully powerful!

I see human connection as having three components. There are the connections we have with others, the feeling of being well connected with ourselves and having a connection with our wider environment and the world. It is when we pause and think about others, or about that big wide world, that we step outside our own bubble and generate empathy, compassion and kindness. It is during these moments of awareness that there is a world out there, spinning around us, that we acknowledge being a part of something bigger, allowing us to gain a deeper sense of meaning and purpose in our lives.

Let's think about these three components of human connection in a little more detail.

Connections with others

Humans are social beings, which doesn't mean we love to party all the time! Being social means that we get a lot out of close relationships, support networks, group activities and mutual hobbies. Through this, we learn worthwhile social skills such as cooperation, empathy and trust, which in turn increase our oxytocin levels. Oxytocin is the hormone associated with positive interactions and bonding, making us feel happier from the inside out. Research shows that social connection reduces the occurrence of mental ill health such as anxiety and depression, enhances emotion regulation, raises immunity and even longevity of life! Being connected with other people creates a feedback loop of psychological and physical wellbeing (Seppala, 2017).

Some of us achieve human connection through prominence in the community or having an active social life with grand friendship groups. For others however, life like this would be more stressful than beneficial and at the quieter end of the spectrum, simply having one person they feel able to confide in is key to their long term mental health. Whether they be the life and soul of a party or the inward thinker, when people are truly allowed to be themselves and connect in ways that are meaningful to them, happiness ensues.

You may have completed one of the many personality profiles available online, or perhaps delved deeper to get a more formal assessment of "who you are". Whether you believe these tools are accurate or unhelpfully putting people into prescribed boxes, there's some value in understanding ourselves and exploring our characteristics, recognising similarities and differences in the traits of others, with a view to flexing and adapting our own style to enhance communication, interactions and improve relationships. I don't know many people who wouldn't want to "do relationships" well, and being more aware of ourselves is one of the ways we can achieve that. In addition, people just love to learn about themselves and personality profiling is fun, at the very least.

This topic is huge, but for now I'll just mention what is possibly the most well known spectrum within personality type theory, which was popularised by Swiss psychoanalyst Carl Jung in the 1920s: extraversion and introversion. Jung believed that extraverts gain energy from external sources, such as spending lots of time around lots of people. At the other end of the spectrum, introverts find such encounters draining of their energy and require alone time to recuperate. Don't be mistaken, both extraverts and introverts enjoy socialising and to complicate matters further, the terms "shy extravert" and "outgoing introvert" are used to describe people who don't fall so neatly into these categories.

Like many topics within the science of mind and behaviour (aka psychology), it's often more complex than it first appears. That's the beauty of being human. That's not to say we can't learn about and understand ourselves better. I urge that we ought to be doing this from a young age which would set us up for a smoother adulthood. Get that on the school curriculum! The point here is that your personality type will in part determine how you like to form and maintain connections, what you need from others and how your relationships thrive and flourish. Different people need different things, the trick is to listen closely enough to your own heart, intuition and conscience to know what makes you feel great. No two human beings will need exactly the same things in their connections, but one thing is for certain, all human beings need one another in some way.

What about "dependence"? There's a word that gets bad press. It's an insult hurled to call someone dependent, reliant and needy. There are human life gurus out there pleading with us to be independent and self sufficient as this somehow makes for a fully functioning, safe human being, protected from the adversities in life somehow by this impenetrable force field that is self reliance. I may be missing something here but I'm yet to understand how this makes us safe, exactly? Surely the negative life events that are somewhat inevitable for us all (such as loss, bereavement and ill health) don't bounce off this imaginary brick wall, do they? The Dalai Lama views happiness as inextricably linked with other people's efforts and cooperation. I take this to mean that depending on one another is okay, in fact, it's a good thing. It certainly isn't bad or weak as some of our human life gurus may have us believe.

The word "needy" is used negatively but that is merely semantics. Think about it for a moment; what an honour to be needed. Wouldn't that be one of the greatest gifts in life; to be so very important to someone else that they feel as though their life wouldn't be the same without you in it. What a tremendous legacy you'd leave if you allowed others to need you. Although, if you're going to be needed, then you probably ought to allow yourself to need others too. This is all in the interest of fairness and balance after all. I certainly need other people in my life and if anyone ever tells me that they need me, I'll puff up with pride in the knowledge that I matter so much to them in that moment. There's a reason that poet John Donne is so often quoted for enlightening us to the fact that, "no man is an island."

For us to find joy through others is an honour. It's also inevitable. Society has begun telling us that we shouldn't need anyone else to be happy. I agree that it's great to love ourselves first, but these are not mutually exclusive. Humans are social animals, they seek mates, their tribe, companions, they even make commitments for life – all with other humans! That's a pretty clear need, if you ask me. We're even born needy. Infants need their carers and I don't know about you but I've never stopped needing mine. I also need to feel loved. Is that bad? A life without the guarantee of people, family, friends and loved ones would be grossly unfulfilling to most of us. I'm okay with being dependent on others when I'm sad or need some help, or when I'd like company to experience life's treasures with. It's a privilege when others need me too. I'm not alone in this either, with the rise of communities that exist with the sole aim of bringing people together to live more meaningful and connected lives, such as the Good Life Project.

So next time someone tells you that they need you, take it as one of the biggest compliments they can give and feel free to tell them you need them too. Or, keep pushing for independence if this hasn't convinced you otherwise, but take a moment to consider why you need to be self reliant. (Did I just use the word "need"?)

Connection with the world

If human connections have such a profound impact on our wellbeing, what's so important about connecting with the environment? To point out the obvious, without nature, we cease to live. Nature is literally essential for our survival and the more aware we are of this, the more connected we feel. With the rise in technology, social media and that sense of not having enough time, it's easy for us to forget what's really important. Humans are designed to spend much more time outdoors than we do nowadays. Even when we are outside, there's often a device in our hands that we're staring down at, because for some reason that we struggle to explain, it seems more pressing in that moment to scroll through the profile of someone we've never met to find out what they ate for their last three meals. We simultaneously miss the birds in the trees, the deer looking at us from the field or the cute passerby who would otherwise have smiled sweetly in our direction!

We are fortunate that the world is there for us, whenever we need it. It asks for nothing in return but that doesn't mean we oughtn't offer something back, for being there for us throughout our entire lives, unconditionally. If you had a person who treated you as well as the environment treats you, you'd return your kindness and be eternally grateful. We take our planet for granted and that's an incredible shame. The good news is that it's never too late to make changes in your attitude and behaviour. Even small alterations can have a fantastic impact. We are all capable and every single one of us has the potential to make a difference. We have so much power for good. It begins with educating ourselves and simply becoming more aware of the consequences of our actions, both good and bad. I'm so glad that scientists in the field of environmental conservation are working tirelessly to find new ways to help look after our wonderful planet. Recycling, reducing our carbon footprint, cycle to work schemes, reducing the use of aerosols, saving paper, water and energy, reducing the production of single use plastics, cleaning up our oceans. We can take it upon ourselves to set up community clean ups, raise awareness, start a compost heap, build a beehive or bug house, layer up and turn the heating down, batch cook our meals, grow our own veg, create habitats for wildlife, use low energy lightbulbs. Thankfully, the potential is endless and it's easy for us to start making a difference right away. Imagine leaving this world at a ripe old age, with a legacy of doing good for the planet. There are few things that are more important, actually, because as I said earlier, without it, we cease to live.

Connection with yourself

Social and environmental interactions are not the only ways we can improve our connections. Spending quality time with ourselves is also vital to mental wellbeing. Allowing ourselves time to slow down, be still and quiet, do less, stop rushing around and step away from those racing thoughts or growing to-do lists is so very important. For some, this is an opportunity to let go of the humdrum of busyness and immerse into a full blown meditation session! For others it's simply taking the time to just be. Either way, it has a fantastic impact on wellness. Why? Quality time alone enables our brains to take time out from all the hard work we employ it to do every day. Even the most relentlessly impressive and central organ of our nervous system deserves some rest and relaxation. Time alone also helps us to identify what matters to us. For example, what is meaningful to us as individuals, what our emotions are telling us, what our strengths and values are. It sounds silly but we often don't really understand ourselves very well at all. Spending time learning about ourselves means that we can make sure we're making the right decisions for wellbeing. Once we begin to do this, we can nurture our wellbeing day to day and spend our time exactly as we want to spend it.

This is possibly one of the most significant mindset shifts a human can have; the realisation that time never comes back for a second chance, so we need to be spending it purposefully. As the American author Annie Dillard beautifully put it, "how we spend our days, is of course, how we spend our lives."

These three components of connection are all connected within themselves too. Helping my friends and family to feel good is a deep source of joy in my life. Why? Because the world we perceive is dependent upon our mind's lens. The world and the mind are interlinked. Our state of mind affects the world (at least, as we experience it), because our "reality" is made up of all we believe and perceive to exist. So, making my loved ones smile gives me a sense of a more decent world, whereby I am able to help others see that decent world too. Having studied a couple of philosophy modules during my first degree, I occasionally ponder such things. Without our view of the world, it cannot exist, so we owe it to this extraordinary planet to do the best we can to perceive it positively in our mind's eye. Our world is what we make of it. No human being ought to sit back and say that they don't have a hand in a better future.

I believe that cultivating deeper connections will create a wider movement to a better world, full of people who genuinely feel they're in it together, for the long run. A shift away from the independent bubbles we find ourselves in and towards appreciating and behaving for the greater good, beginning with our communities and spreading globally.

This is what I hope for in the future.

We can all be part of this movement.

A QUIET MIND

What is mindfulness?

What's this thing called mindfulness that everyone's talking about? Is it just a craze?

Actually, people have been enjoying mindfulness for centuries. Eastern cultures embrace it and I had my first taste of watching the mindfulness gurus do their thing when I was traveling around South East Asia in the early 2000s. I'd never before been in the presence of so many groups, moving more slowly, intentionally, as if they weren't in as much as a rush. That was just the local people going about their daily lives. Inside the temples it was another level of calm. A sea of orange cloth, denoting monks in service to their religion. The senses invigorated with the smell of incense, the sound of collective chanting, the sight of splendour and the feeling of cold stone on my bare feet. This world was peaceful, slow, moving with purpose and meaning. There was nothing to distract your mind from the current circumstance, which was to sit, feel and be. It made me understand why people in this part of the continent seemed so cool and collected, with their slower pace of life and hushed temperaments.

At mealtimes, I'd meet with friends that I'd made and

attempt to order from the menu as they taught me enough words to have a go. The food would come when it came, perhaps our meals were timed together, perhaps not. Dishes were placed in the middle and shared. There were no knives and forks. Only spoons and chopsticks, which forced away the habit of shovelling food into your mouth, to a healthier rate. I remember purposefully pausing to put my cutlery down as I noticed that their custom was to have a bite or two, then rest. Ease back into your chair, relax, talk, listen. There really was no rush.

The same realisation occurred the first time I arrived early for a scheduled excursion. I had booked a trip to Kanchanaburi, a couple of hours north of Bangkok. I was keen to go because my grandad had been a prisoner of war there and endured such unimaginable trauma that I wanted to be where he'd been, perhaps see the landscape he'd cast his eyes over, maybe even walk the same paths. I felt my patience waning as I waited at the allotted location and the pick up time passed. More and more minutes went by and I began to assume this trip wasn't happening. Then, a Thai man on a moped pulled up beside me and gave me a toothy grin, his big brown eyes asking if I was ready to go. I showed him my slip of pink paper that read, "Kanchanaburi one" and he nodded, offered to take my backpack, popped it on the front of his moped and gestured for me to sit on the back. He took me around a few corners, via a couple of stops to say "Sawat Di Khap" to his friends en route, then finally to my next destination – the minibus. Here, there were more backpackers dismounting mopeds and handing their bits of paper to the driver. Another friendly Thai gent looking like he had all the time in the world. It was unusual, but pleasant. This is the way I found transport to work during my time over there. It always turns out okay in the end and it always offers you the opportunity to practise your patience. It made an impression. There was more time to pause, look around and smile. I grew to love it.

A few months later, when I returned home (with quite the

bang as life's pace quickened up in an instant), I set about finding one of those "job things". I worked for a dialectical behaviour therapy service for people with borderline personality disorder and mindfulness was one of the methods embedded into their treatment programme. Finally, I could get my teeth into it, because I had to apply mindfulness every day, as part of my job. At first I was slightly disgruntled that I experienced no guiding beam of light, nor did I levitate as I sat cross legged. I quickly realised it wasn't about that. It was more about centring myself and freeing myself of assumptions. Just like the ones I'd made about how mindfulness would feel.

Put simply, mindfulness is being aware of what's going on in this very moment … it's getting back in touch with how our bodies and minds are feeling without getting caught up in intrusive or negative thoughts or worries. It heightens the sights, sounds, smells and other sensations that pass us by because we're not attending to them when we're trying to do a hundred things at once. Which is the way we are living our lives at the moment, in this busy era where we've become addicted to speed, getting things done and doing them fast. We often feel there isn't enough time to do the things we need to do. So how on earth are we meant to make time for slowing down and being mindful?! The thing is, it's essential that we do, otherwise we'll do ourselves more harm in the long run and our bodies and minds will stop us in any case, by becoming ill and forcing us to take that much needed break. Mindfulness helps us to take those breaks, little and often, proactively and protectively.

Mindfulness helps

When we're being mindful, we begin to enjoy the world around us more, we understand ourselves better, we notice more quickly when we're starting to feel troubled and need to seek support, we look at the world with a fresh pair of eyes, gain a healthier perspective on our circumstances and become more aware of our thoughts, emotions and behaviours. It helps us let go of tricky issues and be more grateful and accepting of what is and of what we have. A mindful brain is better able to handle stress and anxiety and is less prone to depression. It engages the parasympathetic nervous system, which controls digestion and relaxation, conserving energy and lowering our heart rate when we're safe and content. It also engages the neo-cortex, involved in higher order brain functions such as perception, decision making and language. Mindfulness therefore elicits a calmer physiological state and creates mental space for reasonable thinking and effective problem solving (Valikhani et al., 2019).

There's an enormous amount of research and data speaking to all of these benefits, but I'm a fan of giving it a go and experiencing it first hand. That's how we truly engage with something and believe in it, and that's how we become motivated to stick to our endeavours.

Being more mindful

First, you have to want to do it; it's not for everyone but it is really effective if you're up for it. Here are my own top tips for nurturing the calm and watchful master within:

Simply notice. Whatever you're doing, whether talking, walking, eating, or doing housework, notice the small things you're experiencing through all of your senses: smells, sounds, sights, touch, tastes … Do it alongside something relaxing, like enjoying a cuppa, yoga or walking. Try it now. Listen to the sounds around you, focus on the words on the page, how does any quiet space feel? Or gaze at something different for a few seconds – perhaps out of a nearby window or at a plant or ornament in the room. Notice the design, colours, size, movement, shadows or anything that comes to your attention. By doing this, you're giving your brain a break from all other distractions and allowing it to pause, rest, stop for a moment. In fact, our brains aren't designed to multi-task – this is a myth. At best we can merely rapidly switch our attention from one thing to another and back again, which means we're not really attending to anything particularly well when we think we're multi-tasking. So simply notice. Whatever it may be.

Exercise mindfulness often. Just like any other training of any other muscle, our brains (which are organs rather than muscles but work in similar ways) will work better when we practise regularly. Neurotransmitters pass chemical messages around our brains by firing actively between synapses. The more we use them, the more effective they become.

The author and psychologist Rick Hanson (2020) states that, "neurons that fire together, wire together." You can change the neurochemistry and functionality of your brain, to create more calmness and contentment. Choose a time and place that works for you, so that you can embed it as part of your daily routine without too much effort. Some researchers claim that it takes a mere 21 days to form a habit, and just 2 minutes a day can work in creating a new routine. That's got to be worth it for lifelong change and benefits to overall wellbeing. In any case, people often report that they feel better and calmer in the moment. By embedding mindfulness into something you already do each day, you're much more likely to remember to do it and to stick to it. Eventually it will be as commonplace as getting dressed and brushing your teeth. Why not do those things mindfully anyway?!

Do your best to release the pressure. Don't get caught up in what it should feel like, and don't reprimand yourself if thoughts keep rushing in. That's natural. Simply notice those thoughts are there and let them pass by as much as you can. Like watching clouds float along the sky, they're there but they're not sticking and you don't have to control them, just notice them and let them pass. If it helps, name the thoughts as they come in (e.g., "there's my judgement about how I should have done better on that test yesterday"; "I see that you're there, and I'm letting you pass by" or even "I know you need my attention but that will come later"). Sometimes it helps to give a thought the attention it needs as it pops up, especially if it's one of those pesky little persistent blighters, and then let it go. The most important thing is not to judge yourself, nor be hard on yourself, if you're struggling to calm your thoughts. Just do what you can and notice whatever is coming up for you. Your mindfulness experiences won't all be the same and they won't all be smooth. That's okay.

Focus on the now. This is the beauty of mindfulness, really letting go of the past and the future, because the only real moment is this moment right now. We can't change what's already happened nor can we predict or control what will happen later. So to rest on the present moment is the most healthy and calm thing we can do. It really is the only thing we can do, if you think about it. The Dalai Lama professes that, "There are only two days that nothing can be done. One is called yesterday and the other is called tomorrow, so today is the right day to love, believe, do and mostly live."

Name things, non-judgementally. Take some time to look around you, ideally whilst on the move. List all the things you see, without labelling them any further than simply what they're called. This brings your attention into your immediate surroundings and helps you to focus on the facts rather than your biases. A cloud, a tree and a bird are just those, without being labelled as moody, gnarly or noisy. Don't think; simply state all as it is. If you like, explore being non-judgementally aware with your other senses too. Touch things around you and state with a single word what you feel. Name the sounds or even the silence. Step out of thinking and step into the present through your senses.

Just breathe. If nothing else, simply pausing to focus on a few deep, slow breaths will help get you into a mindful frame of mind. Some days are just too darn hard to focus, stop our racing thoughts, sit still … So we just go back to basics and create a foundation for next time, when we're able to engage in it a little better. We focus on breathing and don't concern ourselves with anything else. Breathing is something we do naturally and all the time, of course. Focusing on it can feel a little odd at first. Again, it's not about controlling the breath as such, but some practices involve counting out our breaths, slowing them down, or holding our breath for short periods of time. Find whatever works for you. A common method is to inhale to a count of 6, hold for a few seconds, then exhale to a count of 8, then hold for a few seconds. Exhaling for longer and inhaling for shorter periods enables activation of the parasympathetic nervous system (the rest and digest system, the one that enables us to feel calm by flooding our brain and body with happy chemicals such as oxytocin). A slightly easier way is to slow down your breathing, inhaling and exhaling longer than you normally would, ideally right down into the belly rather than our normal shallow chest breaths. This decreases your heart rate and again, activates the calming system that makes us feel better.

On our most difficult days, even that can feel too much and on those days, we simply breathe. As normal. But we stop for long enough to notice it.

In a nutshell, decide on a time and place that will give you the best chance of forming your mindfulness habit, and decide what you feel motivated to do and believe will work. Release the pressure of what it should feel like; just be in the moment and let everything else go.

Do it often. Last but not least, enjoy it.

PART TWO: REACH UP

FLOW

What is flow?

The definition of flow is "the action or fact of moving along in a steady, continuous stream". In psychological terms, flow refers to a state in which we are fully immersed in an activity, feeling focused, involved and in the zone. One of the founders of the positive psychology movement, Mihály Csikszentmihalyi, is a happiness researcher following his experience of being a Second World War prisoner during his childhood. He proposes that the best moments in our lives are not the passive times, but the times when our bodies and minds are stretched voluntarily in an effort to accomplish something worthwhile. People are simply happiest during flow. We lose track of time, feel less self conscious and are devoid of interfering thoughts or worries. Usually, the activity we are immersed in is enjoyable, intrinsically rewarding and there is a balance between the level of skill we possess and the level of challenge we feel when engaging in it. This balance of skill and challenge is often referred to as the "flow zone" or "flow channel". If something feels like too much of a challenge compared to our level of skill, then we experience worry, anxiety and stress, which disrupt our ability to reach a state of flow. Conversely, if our skill level is way above the level of challenge, then we experience boredom, demotivation and apathy.

Take dancing as an example. This is one of my longest standing hobbies, so I find it easy to draw parallels when I consider the different phases of flow. When I joined my very first dance class, I had no idea what to expect, nor did I know what I was doing. Of course, with 28 years of growing up under my belt, I had a wealth of experience on dance floors, albeit more of the "throwing random shapes" kind, without the need to account for where my limbs were or whether I was doing it well! This comes with its own kind of flow, which I admit I still get excited about. When it came to joining a "proper" partner dance class, I listened hard to the instructors, did my best to get my limbs in order and follow the patterns of movements with the added layer of another person, their limbs and movements! At first, my skill was significantly lower than the challenge, so whilst I thoroughly enjoyed myself, I wasn't in flow just yet. I was working hard to get it right and this came with mental effort. This raised my skill level and so the flow came later. Once I'd mastered the art of following my leader and responding to movements and music intuitively, I reached that state of total immersion. I stopped having to consciously think about dancing and it became natural, almost effortless although still with enough challenge to require my absolute attention and commitment. Time flew by, I thought about nothing else on the dance floor and loved every minute. I also progressed in my ability, getting better with practice.

Flow for wellbeing

If all this doesn't sound good enough, there's something else that occurs when we're in flow, which is possibly the most important factor and why I believe we need to give this concept more attention in our lives. Flow improves wellbeing. When I dance, I forget my troubles. It's like a holiday for my mind; I truly step away from my to-do list, the chores I haven't done and that problem I'm yet to solve. After dancing, I have a huge sense of achievement, a smile on my face and tend to sleep better. Having one or two activities that we know will transcend us into the zone means we can draw upon those when we need them and know that we always have an escape – a treat for the mind! There are endless activities that will lead us into flow, so we need to find what works for us. We're all different and so I can't tell you what you need to get out there and do, but I guarantee there will be many options. You're probably already aware of what some of those options are and they're not always physical or come under the banner of exercise. Reading, watching a movie, walking in the woods can all put us into that same wonderful mindset. It's not even restricted to the extracurricular. Study and work bring plenty of opportunities for flow too. Peak moments of total absorption and optimal states of consciousness work wonders to heighten our creativity, productivity and performance.

The brain in flow

Researchers are becoming increasingly interested in this salubrious state of being. Prefrontal cortex activity is reduced in times of flow, which is the brain region associated with conscious and explicit thinking and complex cognitive functions. Some theorists hypothesise that the temporary inactivation of the prefrontal cortex is responsible for lowering self consciousness and hushing our inner critic – that unhelpful voice telling us we can't do it or we're doing it wrong (Dietrich, 2004). Moreover, the subconscious mental processes are given the space and freedom to engage with other parts of the brain that are often dampened by our conscious thoughts. Dopamine, which is one of our happy hormones associated with the approach to a reward, is thought to be related to flow (Gruber et al., 2014). This is why we feel more motivated, creative and curious during flow. How magnificent that we can bring this about ourselves, by choosing to spend time on the right activities.

Some of us like to understand the science behind what's happening, which gives us the impetus to make changes in our lives. Some of us don't care much about the reasons behind it, just so long as it feels good! Either way, whatever you're doing, if you have enough skill to make it there, with just enough challenge to maintain your interest, you can dive right into the flow channel and stay there for as long as you need to, whether it's to complete that task or boost your happiness.

AWE IN NATURE

There is a word that's perhaps overused; that word is "awesome". The definition is "a feeling of great admiration or respect, sometimes coupled with surprise". It can stop us in our tracks. When we spy a unique view, at a lakeside, in some woodland, beneath a waterfall, on the edge of the coast, when watching the sunrise, moon rise, sunset, or a sky full of stars in the middle of nowhere. Awe has an instant impact on our mental state and a fantastic one at that.

A nature boost

Research shows that spending just 2 hours a week in nature boosts our serotonin and oxytocin levels (White et al., 2019) and is associated with good overall health and psychological wellbeing. We already know how magical oxytocin is. Serotonin is linked to mood and desire, a deficiency of which can lead to depression. Taking a walk in the sunshine is known to boost serotonin, lifting our mood in turn. Nature is healing; it helps us balance our work and leisure time which helps reduce stress and burnout. It doesn't matter whether this is a 2-hour stomp in the woods or several 10-minute hops to the local park, people who spend 2 hours or more each week wandering around green or blue space feel significantly better for it. The key is to immerse yourself in natural scenes and be mindful, so let nature be the goal and nothing else. Switch everything else off – your devices and your thinking – and allow your five senses to take in whatever the world is offering to you while you're out there.

Humans were designed to spend much more time in nature than we do nowadays, with the rise in technology and social media, which of course have their place. It's important to strike the right balance for you. By being more mindful about the time you're spending online, staring at a screen, communicating with a device or scrolling through words and pictures that mean nothing to you in reality, you can make conscious decisions about what's adding value and what's sapping your energy. Making a little effort to step away from those screens in favour of more fresh air time, on your own or with others, talking to people, noticing the world around you, engaging all your senses, gives your mind (and your eyes) a rest.

It facilitates a feeling of connection to something bigger than your own bubble. It doesn't take much, perhaps switching off a few of those notifications, or unsubscribing to a few of those emails, only connecting with, befriending and following online contacts that bring you joy. Or even turning it all off and leaving it behind when you step outdoors to go for that stroll. Start looking up more than looking down. Gaze into the distance once more, rather than at that nearby screen in the palm of your hand. If you make small changes such as these, it'll undoubtedly have an impact on your sense of time, energy and freedom. Not to mention your happiness.

The impact of awe

Why is awe so, well, awesome?! When we reach the summit of a mountain and a vast horizon of sheer space comes into view. When we catch the sunset as it lights the endless sky with oranges and reds. When we see a bright moon and a billion stars in the unreachable sky, staring up at them staring down at us. Why is it so breathtaking? It's because it defies our day to day experience. It challenges our sense of reality. It connects us to something greater than ourselves. Everything else going on in our lives (stress, concern, even time) becomes insignificant in that moment … and we become limitless.

Michiel van Elk, a researcher at the University of Amsterdam, found that the experience of awe reduces rumination and over thinking about all those items on our stress list (Elk et al., 2019). This lovely emotion increases activity in the fronto-parietal network (a brain area involved in externally directed attention) and brings us out of thinking selfishly by immersing us into our surroundings and the wider world. This goes some way to explain why awe inspires generosity and connection towards others. Allowing more awe experiences into our daily lives helps dissolve our ego (our self narrative that we build based on unhelpful assumptions and thinking traps) and transcends us into a state of mindfulness or flow.

Awesome people

Let's think a moment more about connection. There's something magical that happens when two humans are in the same space, concentrating on one another. People can be awe-inspiring and rewarding because each and every individual is amazing in their own right, for reasons we may only see if we spend quality time engaging with and listening to them. Humans are literally awesome! Can you think of a time when you felt that great admiration and respect for a person? Or a time when someone surprised you in a way that made you stop and notice how much you appreciate them? This feeling of awe comes from those real life moments between us. It's so easy to miss if we're studying a filtered photograph of what the neighbour had for breakfast three days ago. Sometimes it's good to pause and check in with ourselves on what's really important in our lives. It's completely within your control how much time you allow yourself to spend scrolling through other people's news and how much time you spend seeking out real life awe.

One of my strongest awe memories involving both nature and people is of a time during a work trip to the British Virgin Islands, following the devastation that category 5 Hurricane Irma left in its wake. The small islands were obliterated. Homes flattened, infrastructure demolished, belongings scattered and lost forever. Hours of unimaginable fear amidst the strongest winds throwing everything up into the air and taking roofs off houses, sandwiched between the preceding days of anticipation, waiting to learn whether the storm would bypass or hit and the subsequent, quiet realisation that everything had changed in an instant. Everything. Except the people. Those awesome people.

I was asked to travel out to the islands to offer mental health aid to survivors. Miraculously, their fatalities were low. For a month, I worked long days seeing as many people on the islands as possible, in order to have as much of a positive impact as I could manage during that time. Intrusive thoughts told me I couldn't possibly make a significant difference, but I sure as heck wanted to try. I spent days preparing for the unique trip, researching everything I could about natural disasters, hurricanes and post trauma support. I arrived in the middle of the night, in the dark, greeted at the minute airport on Tortola and chauffeured by boat to Virgin Gorda, which would be my home. Tired from the travelling, I didn't spend long exploring my surroundings, particularly upon learning that the doors didn't lock because the apartment was, of course, hurricane damaged. In the darkness, in a new place, far from home and by myself, knowing that any passerby could get inside if they wanted to, it's safe to say that first night wasn't my best sleep. Awoken by a cockerel at 5am, I blearily moved around the apartment, its water stained walls, boarded windows, resident bugs and gecko. There was a roof and the water was running, so I was grateful. I got myself ready for work, thinking that all my preparation and research would be what benefitted people most … of course, it wasn't.

It turns out that people, human beings, want and need something much simpler in moments of despair. They want to have the opportunity to express themselves freely, to be raw and real. They want to be heard and understood. They want to feel held, metaphorically at least. Human connection, vulnerability and authentic compassion were all I needed in my suitcase.

I had the privilege of working on Tortola, Gorda, Mosquito and Necker Island, spending time with Sir Richard Branson, his wife and colleagues, as well as the islanders in their communities. Richard invited me to venture out with him on various hikes, cycle rides and boat trips. I even shared my chips with him at dinner (truth be known, he stole them when I wasn't looking!). He was intrigued about my work and my life and made me feel like a valued member of the team, not to mention his social circle whilst I was there. That will always be a highlight of my career and I count myself incredibly fortunate.

An equal highlight was the experience that blindsided me completely, one that I hadn't anticipated, let alone planned for. It was the immersion into a world of people who were utterly awesome (now understanding the gravitas of that word and all its glorified meaning). Most of my time wasn't spent discussing the aftereffects of a hurricane, but all of the day to day matters that humans have to deal with the world over, because of that thing called life, no matter who we are, where we're from or what we do. How astonishing. I fully respect the confidentiality of every single person I met, so I'll simply say that we really are all so very similar in the mere fact that we're humans with bodies, minds, experiences and emotions alongside likes, dislikes, needs, scars, hopes and fears. I didn't bother taking my folder on natural disasters and PTSD with me the following day. I just took my sensitivity, vulnerability and authenticity and hoped it would be enough.

I've never had such rewarding feedback in my working life. And I'm not taking credit, it was all down to them. The people I met were hopeful, optimistic, resilient and held faith, even after all they'd been through. Living away from their loved ones because some had managed to flee and others hadn't escaped in time, or because their homes, schools and workplaces no longer existed. Clearing rubble and beginning the drawn out process of rebuilding. Knowing that hurricanes happen and they may go through it all again someday and who knows when. Never have I had so many moments of realising what the important things in life really are. People. Nature. Just being.

One chap by the name of Cumbar, a taxi driver born and raised on the islands, agreed to tell his story about the aftermath of the hurricane as one I could openly share. He said,

"It was a life changing experience, I wish for nobody to see. Three days after, I had the opportunity of going to Road Town. Seeing Road Town, I was sick to my stomach. It was just like a garbage heap. A lot of work was done and we're seeing some small progress taking place. Seeing all of the devastation, we were wondering if we were going to ever get back to where we were. But with the resilience of the individuals here and the help from outsiders, we're grateful, we're working hard and trying to make sure we get back. People like yourself who visit, it's all about seeing you leave with as big a smile that you came with. It's all about people. People are the fullness of this life that we do live and at the end of the day, when you can make somebody who comes to our territory leave with as big a smile as they came with, it makes you feel like you earn a million. I enjoy doing what I do. Life's journey is a little too short to do things that you don't enjoy. What I enjoy is when I can make somebody smile. And you who haven't been here before, I want to welcome you to the BVI. We're here in the aftermath of the hurricane, but it's beautiful and it's going to get better, so come on down man. Bless and love."

I don't know about you, but I was bowled over by how little he ruminated on the awful impact of that natural disaster. Instead, he quickly moved on to the positives. The message of re-building and the sense of growth. He was focused on what he could do to help others. Even though, on our journey in his taxi, he had described to me how his wife had been trapped with their baby in their house. That they could only communicate for a time via telephone because he was on a different island working. How, once the hurricane had stolen their communication channel and brought down the telegraph poles, all he could do was hope that his family were alive and safe. In those moments, he explained how he only wanted them not to worry and his sense that, because he knew her soul, she would have the strength to be okay. Once they were re-united, it turned out that they had both been having the same thoughts and feelings about one another. Somehow, amidst the trauma, they held faith and maintained hope. Utter resilience. This happened time and time again with every person I met. It astounded me. I say it again, humans are awesome. There's a video of Cumbar and I on my social media channels, if you'd like to see this wonderful soul. If you ever visit and have the fortune to meet him, please give him a huge hug from me and give him your biggest smile, it'll make his day, no matter what.

Awesome sights

I could talk for a long while about my short time in the British Virgin Islands. It's safe to say they will always hold a very special place in my heart. One final reflection I'd like to share is a particular moment when I stood looking out to sea one evening at sunset, which was my way of de-compressing. I'd just completed my daily yoga session, with the warm sand between my toes and chickens running around on the beach. A common sight. As I gazed out towards the horizon, my vista was one of clear turquoise water lapping gently onto a white beach, with expensive yachts moored and bobbing silently and contently. Every now and then, the odd sailor would appear, or there would be a little blue light cast from their boat. But generally there was little movement or noise. The sun was setting, which threw the clear sky into deep blues and purples, with a hint of orange as the glow of the sun said goodbye for another day. A few of the brightest stars had already made an appearance and glistened gently above the yachts and the waves. The air smelled fresh and was warm with a gentle breeze. It felt like a place that people go to be free and still. In a word – paradise.

With a smile, I inhaled fully and turned around, stopping dead on the spot. The paradox of the sight that was now before me took my breath away. I knew it was there, but I'd forgotten in that previous moment of bliss. As I looked in the opposite direction to where I'd been practising my yogic poses, this time staring inwards towards land, my view was now one of chaos; an aftermath of something harsh.

Randomly strewn were bent and broken pieces of metal and wood, all shapes and sizes, unrecognisable as anything, really. The inner structures of buildings that you don't normally see as they're encased inside the brickwork and plaster, were standing bare between huge piles of rock. The bits that you're not supposed to see because they're not pretty, were on show with nowhere to hide. Scanning the overwhelming scene, it felt like a giant jigsaw puzzle. All the pieces strewn all over the place, with no form or pattern; where nothing yet makes sense and you don't know where to start. I saw partially crushed cars with broken windows, abandoned and useless. Bricks and mortar that were once homes, schools or bars, were broken down as rubble, in piles at the edges of the roads. If the paths could still be seen, they were peppered with shards of glass and metal.

Even the natural elements had taken a hit. Broken trees with brown leaves and no flowers or fruit. Shades of brown across the landscape. Palm trees that looked like they'd been sawn in half, with perhaps a leaf or two remaining, nowhere near as majestic as I was used to seeing them. It made me feel so sorry, so sad for all of it. Everything looked lost and barely alive. In a word – devastation.

I turned around several times in disbelief, taking in the juxtaposition of these two worlds, in the very same place. Things aren't always as they seem. We ought not make assumptions based on what we see, especially if what we see is only from one angle. There are always two sides to every story. Probably more. The highs and lows come together in the same package. The list of these poignant realisations went on and on. I doubt I'll ever forget that moment. That was a moment of intense awe.

Awesome activities

The act of writing about powerful memories transports you back there. That's the power of remembering and shows how important it is to relive the nice ones as often as we can. Back home in the United Kingdom, where hurricanes don't often bother us but other devastating life events do, I recognise the importance of understanding what I need to maintain a healthy lifestyle. What can you do from today to bring more awe into your life? I love wild swimming. In the sea, a lake or river, ideally with trees or cliffs or a horizon, even better at sunrise and sunset (exponentially topping up the awe-o-meter!). Cold water swimming is found to reduce stress, improve circulation, activate endorphins and boost the immune system. It's invigorating, refreshing and connects you with people you're out there with. There's always lots of laughter and a great sense of achievement. It's a fantastic start or end to any day, takes your mind off physical and mental aches and pains. It makes you feel alive.

We spend too much time in our heads, thinking, contemplating, analysing. Nature based activities support more time away from constant thought that makes our minds feel full and weighty. Instead, we experience the world as it is in the moment through all our senses – sight, sound, touch, taste and smell. Try an awe walk, which is a stroll through natural scenery, whereby you intentionally shift your attention outward instead of inward. Studies are showing that just 15 minutes of awe walking each week leads to significant boosts of prosocial emotions such as compassion and gratitude (Sturm et al., 2020).

How can you take it one step further and use those experiences to help others and increase awe in their lives too? Nature based therapy weaves together personal wellness, community improvement and greater sustainability in a nice therapeutic bundle. Often, it involves doing service for nature to build mindfulness, emotional awareness, self efficacy, resilience. Hearts open, relationships flourish and communities thrive as we engage in activities that benefit the greater good. In my mind, this is the way the world should be. This should be our focus.

I'm a huge fan of utilising things we have a natural abundance of to help us feel good and to deepen our connections with our environment. Two things that we have at our fingertips are nature and people. We can help ourselves, help each other and do good things for our planet by connecting more on every one of these levels and appreciating all that is around us, no matter what. It's as simple as that.

Do you know what the best part is? Awe is free, it's everywhere, and it's accessible to us all.

ENJOYMENT

A joyful spirit

Joy, by definition, is feeling of great pleasure and happiness. The American author Elizabeth Gilbert encapsulates the joyful spirit of adventure and writes about how we can each invite more joy into our lives by waking up the creative spirit that lies within us all (Gilbert, 2016). She believes that we internalise negative feedback from our younger days, perhaps the words of a schoolteacher who gave us a harsh grade for our best artwork, then believe right through our adult years that we aren't capable of creating new and wonderful things. We have a sense that we are simply not creative types, or that we don't have a good imagination. This is simply not the case. Humans are born with an immense amount of imagination and creativity which bubbles up in all that we do during infancy – that pastime we call "play". This doesn't go away, we just repress it because we compare ourselves with others and believe we're not good enough. That's where the mistake lies, in that negative belief. It's skewed, as many of our beliefs are. There is so much joy to be found when we dare to open up the boundaries we place on our imagination and let it loose.

Reflecting on joy

My thoughts on this lovely little word are best encapsulated by a journal entry that I wrote a few months after a particularly difficult time. I'll share my journal entry of raw and unfiltered thoughts verbatim, for the sake of this chapter (and of course, for authenticity).

"Something intriguing happened today that I wanted to remember. In the context of the last few months, where I experienced the end of a relationship (one of those 'serious' ones that was meant to last), a significant and potentially life changing operation, and a redundancy from a job that I thought was secure and going places. I felt I had lost everything I had going for me and suddenly it was very hard to see light at the end of the tunnel I'd been plunged into against my will. I began to worry about losing loved ones because that was the only thing I could imagine that could be worse. There's a profound example of negativity bias for you! I hated waking up every day and realising that this was now my life and I simply wished I could live someone else's (which would surely be better!) or hibernate until it all passed without having to go through those groundhog day feelings of struggling through more or less everything. With clarity of mind, we know that there are always people who are much worse off than us, but a clear mind doesn't prevail when we've had enough to knock us into the pit. I simply did not want to go through the grief. Nobody does. It's painful.

On one of the worst days, which ironically happened to be one of the brightest days of that Spring, I was sitting by a river without much else to do that afternoon. I got caught up in how the water fell from rocks of various heights, onto various surfaces, how it crashed, flowed, bubbled, merged, moved, with the sun bouncing off its waves. I guess I was unintentionally being mindful. It was one of the most powerful moments of clarity I can recall having. I suddenly found myself wishing I could be like water. In the way it ebbs and flows without getting caught on anything at all, moving through, over and around anything it its way, without getting stuck, anywhere, on anything. Constantly moving and adapting, merging within itself if it had to, in order to respond freely to whatever the environment offered.

I found myself thinking about how water can be completely still and beautiful or thunderously loud and busy, yet still just as breathtaking, perhaps even more so because it can be both. Water doesn't hold back, it isn't afraid of anything, it doesn't concern itself with what might happen if it shoots headlong into barriers or breakwaters, it just keeps on going with gusto all the time, never looking back. I found myself in awe of its absence of stickiness, its constant fluidity and movement. Yes, I wanted to be like water. Why though? Because it is equally enticing in its calmest and craziest moments. It looks like it's having a jolly good time no matter what, whether steadily meandering or being exhilaratingly fierce. Wouldn't it be fantastic if life could be experienced just like that, and if onlookers could see us in our chaotic moments as enjoying the upheaval where we have no idea which way is up or what we might crash into along the way.

I realised that if water had feelings, it would probably be enjoying itself. And that led me back to reflect on my life and the familiar feeling that I'd lost everything I had and wanted. Of course I hadn't. Because something that's worth more than everything in life is the sheer enjoyment of it. In that moment of pure clarity I became aware that I'd paused the unconscious stream of thinking that takes over us if we don't keep a handle on it. Because of our well developed frontal lobes, we're in danger of over thinking our way into despair and losing track of our very being, our actual selves. Eckhart Tolle (2008) calls this the ego, which is the story we tell ourselves based on our past pains and how we judge ourselves based on external factors. This is separate to our true selves, which he calls our essence or being. The best way out of the ego state is to be present and in the moment. The more present we can be, the less we live in our pasts or futures. The only real moment is now. Consider this: you have thoughts zooming through your mind all the time, thousands every day! The majority of these are believed to be repetitive (therefore arguably pointless) and negative (there's that negativity bias again). Nobody wants that and we ought to get a grip on these little blighters! Imagine rising above yourself and notice that you're having thoughts, or notice that you're observing something in your surroundings. That rising above yourself is rising above the stream of thought and allowing yourself to be more conscious and present. A feeling of calm usually follows.

Thinking about what you could, should or might have rather than focusing on what is with you right now, causes you to suffer. In a nutshell, a lot of suffering is caused by thinking. Repetitively. Negatively. That constant stream of thinking. Another option available to you is to enjoy whatever you're doing or whatever you have, then yours is the life that others envy, you are the one that people strive to be like. There's no envy or incessant desire, because you have joy.

I'd been believing that losing a relationship and losing a job had made me feel unhappy. Yet that relationship and that job had not been making me happy either, for quite some time. So I wasn't loving life either way. It wasn't a case of 'having it' or 'not having it'. It was a case of me not enjoying things as they were, whether life was turning up, down or sideways. And that was in my power to change.

It doesn't matter what or who you have or don't have. All that matters is that you're enjoying it, whatever *it* is."

ACCEPTANCE

This is one of the biggest tasks we can hope to achieve in life. Acceptance can feel like the highest mountain to climb, but at the top, the views are spectacular and from there, the journey becomes easier. Our best shot at this is to practise it, often, with small things in our lives that we can easily accept, even if we'd rather they be different. Then, when bigger struggles emerge, we're well rehearsed in acceptance and can move through to the other side with grace. The need for acceptance can occur when we least expect it, so it's essential that we've got this in our armoury.

The highs

I mentioned that one of the biggest hobbies in my life has been dancing. I've always loved it. There's a video of me before I could talk, rocking from side to side as my parents encouraged me to have a little boogie. A few years older, I'd put on shows and rehearse for hours, pretending to be various protagonists from all manner of movies (Grease being the longest standing performance, naturally). A few years on I was allowed into nightclubs and no matter how tired we were or what time we had to be up the next morning, my dancing feet got the better of me and we were often the last to leave. It was the thrill of being a dancer. I'm often either listening to music or singing in my head, if not out loud, prancing around the house. I find it virtually impossible not to move when a song comes on that I like. It's always been in my bones. In my late twenties I joined a partner dance class because I'd moved to Devon and was eager to meet people and learn how dance, properly this time!

I'll never forget that first class. I walked into the large room and felt like I was entering a different world with the lights down, the music up, a huge wooden floor; the place was filled with people in rows, waiting for the first lesson to begin. Armed with some comfortable shoes, my favourite skirt and a bucket load of enthusiasm, I dived in with both feet. I put down my bag and walked towards the lines of people, with no concept of how significant this hobby was about to become in my life. I introduced myself to people as I changed partners with each new move I learned, making lifetime friends. It was as though I'd been doing this class all my life; me and the dancing just clicked. I was thoroughly enjoying myself. I remember smiling uncontrollably and thinking, with certainty, that this would be a forever hobby.

That feeling of certainty doesn't happen often, but when it does, you really feel it. You don't have to think about it or wonder, you just know. Some weeks I spent more nights dancing than not. It became such an important part of my life that I felt it was part of my identity. True to type, I was always one of the last to leave those classes, with the poor staff trying to clean the floors around me as I chatted to other enthusiasts and continued the energy, right to the last possible moment. It wasn't long before I was putting myself forwards to get involved in any way I could. I became a member of the crew who greeted dancers as they arrived, making sure they felt involved. Others noticed my commitment and I found myself being asked to help on stage as the teacher's demo. I attended national events at weekends and other teachers asked me to be their demo, too. I learned a lot and it led to me becoming a dance teacher myself. I had a dance partner with whom I travelled to all kinds of national and overseas events. We taught a range of classes, performed in dance shows, cabarets and competitions. I adored teaching and retained my love for social dancing. Bringing together music and movement was where I wanted to spend my time. I'd be lost in the moment, in flow, losing track of all else. It was quite magical. My partner and I became well known in the dance world; people would contact us to ask whether we'd be at an event so that they could join us. For the quiet girl from North Staffordshire, it felt like a tiny taste of fame. It got to the point where just walking into a room felt great, seeing smiles from people who'd be keen to swing me around the dance floor and practise the moves we'd taught them. I hardly had a moment to myself during those busiest years, because everyone seemed to know who we were and I was constantly being asked to dance. We featured on videos, DVDs and even created our own choreography. It felt great. It was such a high. I met so many people, some of whom knew me solely as a dance teacher and some of whom became my best friends. It was like a calling; it changed my life.

The lows

One year, my dance partner and I travelled the country and world more than usual, meaning we were away from home every few weeks, but that didn't matter because I was doing what I loved. A dream come true. I was in a long distance relationship at the time and one evening, my boyfriend informed me he was running late, so I should go dancing rather than wait at home. About halfway through the night, I checked my phone to send him a message just as a fellow dancer came over to me and jovially said, "You're here to dance, not rest!" Ironically I was known as someone who hardly left the dance floor. He insisted I dance and I couldn't refuse. He led me to the other end of the floor, I guess it was his preferred spot. At the end of the track, before I could return to my phone, my dance partner appeared and asked me to dance. We were partners for a reason – we connected well, knew each others' moves inside out and had fun.

That particular night, he tried a move with a twist. He led me behind his back and into a very fast, multiple spin, which meant I had no concept of where he was, with the world zooming by as I put full faith into him as my leader. As he turned towards me, spinning around quickly himself, he misjudged the distance and hit me square in the face with his elbow. Brute force as we were both travelling at speed. I heard the crunch and felt instant pain and sickness. We both stopped dead and blood streamed from my nose. It was broken. Other dancers rushed to my aid. One of them drove me to the hospital and the pain was so bad that it hurt to cry. There was nothing they could do because of the swelling. I had to go home and lie on my back with my head elevated slightly, holding in tears, not knowing what my face was going to look like and unable to sleep. I didn't dare look in the mirror. It was horrible. I'll spare the detail of the next few trips to hospital but it wasn't pleasant. The incident meant that I couldn't dance for a few months until I had recovered from corrective surgery. Neither my nose nor my dancing felt right. I struggled for a long time with the reality of those facts. I'd had my nose broken earlier in life, accidentally by a friend whilst playing and being silly. I was very careful with my nose after that, I didn't want a repeat of it, but it happened again. I couldn't believe it.

I had a hard time accepting that certain aspects of my identity had altered in one dramatic incident. I didn't look or feel like myself. A disorienting and disturbing feeling, physically and mentally uncomfortable. In an instant, I went from being at the top of my game with a hobby I adored, my biggest passion and social life attached, to not being able to do it anymore. As soon as I was able to get back onto the dance floor, it didn't feel the same. I was afraid for the first time. Fearful of elbows! Scared of it happening again. I couldn't put my whole soul into it anymore. My dream, my passion, my escape had become dull and disappointing. For a while, when I looked into the mirror I was reminded of that awful incident.

Many emotions surfaced during that time, from sadness to anger, blame and frustration. In hindsight, I understand that this was a process of loss.

The road to acceptance

Thinking back over the chain of events that led to that traumatic incident, how my boyfriend had been running late and suggested I go dancing, how my fellow dancer insisted that he led me to the opposite end of the dance floor where my partner then asked me for that fateful dance. Had any one of those events not occurred, it may never have happened. Or was it meant to be that way? I certainly learned a lot. It was a stark realisation as to how, in the blink of an eye, life could be impacted so greatly. For a while I felt angry, even though I knew that nobody planned it. Blaming didn't help me feel better. Finally, I realised that no matter how much I pushed against it, my new reality was as it was and the best thing I could do was accept it. Plus, of course, gain the perspective that it could have been so much worse. In a lot of ways, I was lucky. This was step one. Step two was getting to the point where I really did accept it. Pretending didn't work. It had to be authentic. I got there, eventually. It took a while, but over time other exciting things emerged, my face was still mine and I still loved dancing, they were just a little different and that was okay. I had a helping hand from a few people who may never even know what a powerful effect they had on me accepting my new self.

Life throws curve balls at us. Sometimes soft and sometimes really hard. Sometimes life's curve balls affect us in ways that seem trivial to someone else. It doesn't matter, it's all relevant. Whatever affects you, affects you and that's that. The task isn't to brush aside difficult feelings because there's always someone worse off. That would mean that none of us could ever be sad or hurt or disappointed. It's okay to feel whatever we feel. The trick is to move through it to a point of truthful acceptance as soon as we possibly can so that we can move forward and move ourselves on. So that we can continue living our wonderful, glorious lives to the full. We must stop, often, to reflect on what we have, for as long as we have it.

We strive to be accepted, included, valued with all our quirks, preferences and foibles. Yet we struggle to accept situations that don't neatly fit into what we desire or have come to expect. The difference between expecting and accepting is immense, as is the outcome of these two states of mind. Expectation, particularly when unmet, often precedes shock, disappointment, frustration and even rage. Acceptance elicits a much calmer, open minded and healthy mindset and experience.

Ideally, acceptance travels in both directions, ideally simultaneously. What I mean is, we can work on accepting others as they are, situations we wouldn't choose and that is our responsibility to put mental effort into. Just as important is the acceptance that flows from others, onto us. Asking for acceptance is one thing, but modelling acceptance is best. Showing that we accept what comes our way and demonstrating how we accept our own idiosyncrasies gives others the chance to deeply respect us for who we are. Sometimes I find playful humour in the smallest things. Other times I'm serious. I accept that these are both a part of who I am. Both are okay. Sometimes all I want to be is alone. Other times it's the last thing I want. Both are okay. I'm independent and capable of looking after myself. I like being cared for and sometimes need a hand with things. Both are okay. One human being can be all these things.

We become overly concerned about matching our behaviour with what we believe to be our identity, trying to pigeonhole ourselves and others into boxes, with neat titles describing our characteristics and traits. At times, this can be extremely useful in understanding ourselves and others, learning the equal value of similarity and difference. My point here is that it's not always neat and tidy, nor does it always make sense. And believe me, I like things to make sense! But people are complex and changeable. They can be confusing and even shocking at times, but it also means we can flex and adapt and most importantly, empathise. As an example, because I recognise and accept that I can both crave and despise being alone, I meet others with compassion when they express their own need for company or solitude. People are complex and simple and both are okay.

Honing acceptance

First, put down that need for control of everything out there. It's unnecessary in most cases as the only control we really have is over ourselves, our own mindset, responses and behaviour. Everything else is in control of itself. Surely that's the way it should be? To me, that seems fair. Realising this is a huge leap forwards and a great relief, for a start! Imagine not having to worry about anything other than yourself, what you think and what you do. So much of our worry can be released. Relinquishing control over situations and people also allows alternative opportunities to emerge, new possibilities that we may never have created ourselves, had we claimed full control. Not only is it easier to let some of that go, but more often than not, things tend to work out. The world has a funny way of ironing out its own creases, if we let it. Looking back on some of the times I've tried to control a situation because I felt I had to, or that I knew best, or that it would all fall to pieces if I didn't, I realise the mental strain I put myself under unnecessarily, when in many instances Doris Day had it right when she sang, "whatever will be, will be".

You are where you are and no matter what, you are more "okay" than "not okay". Always. This is because being healthy and successful all the time is simply impossible. Sometimes, life is just plain hard, heartbreaking, tough, painful and unfair. That's okay too, because it's normal. As long as we accept that is the case. Not accepting is what causes emotional turmoil, distraction, mental and physical illness. So no matter what it is, no matter how gut-wrenchingly, catastrophically hopeless you feel, know that it's a part of being human. You're not the only one who's been dragged through the mud and you're not the only one going through it right now. It's a part of your contract with life, as it is for us all.

Radical acceptance

What is life anyway? It is a bunch of cells, merged together to form what we call a body, functioning well (mostly) hopefully for a good many years on this earth. Miraculous as this is (and I don't profess to truly understand the extraordinary feat that is human existence), it doesn't stop there. Those cells have a whale of a time buzzing around in their bodily armour in the wider world. The wider world is full of more of these bunches of cells. These cells and their inhabitant bodies react to their surroundings and events that happen around them and this forms a spectrum of experiences and memories over the years, which we look back on and call our "life". Mental health is the result of how we view those events, our reactions to the happenings and experiences … are we all following? What I'm getting at here is that all of this "stuff" is going to happen, whether we like it or not. Radical acceptance of that spectrum of experiences and understanding that life is as it is and we're bloomin' fortunate to have been granted this bunch of cells, is actually where good mental health is at.

Remember the quote by L. R. Knost earlier? Life is amazing, then it's awful and in between times it's mundane … yet all breathtakingly beautiful (I paraphrase). We can apply this sentiment to people too. They're wonderful, they're also difficult and can push our buttons as much as we push theirs. Yet we are all in this together and overall, we need those people, even the ones that frustrate the heck out of us at times. Nothing is smooth, nobody is plain. Where would be the fun in that? When we accept, we let go of those difficult feelings and everything feels a little calmer. After all, adapting ourselves and the way we respond to everything and everyone on the planet is a darn sight easier and more achievable than trying to change everything and everyone else instead!

Refuse to blame

One of the largest causes of stress today is relationships. Ironically. Because relationships are also one of the largest precursors to happiness. There's a huge difference then between healthy and unhealthy relationships, or perhaps it's all about how we think and behave within the relationships that we have. It's safe to say that most of us have experienced a bad break up at some point, one that just didn't end well.

At the point of demise, an easy response is to apportion blame as to why it went so wrong, especially when there was so much promise to begin with. What's healthier? To blame ourselves and live with the belief that we did something wrong and therefore are somehow incapable of "doing" relationships? To blame the ex-partner, which sits uncomfortably because that possibly means they're blaming us in return. Or to blame the world for dishing out such a rotten situation for us, but that only leaves a sour taste in our mouths for the miracle that is being alive and we certainly don't want that! It feels utterly rubbish any which way, right? So how about we blame nobody, blame nothing and see a bad breakup as normal. That way, we can love the world, accept our own unique way of "doing" relationships and think kindly towards our exes as they move on.

Maybe we don't see relationships as broken at all, even if they do end, because they taught us something and made us who we are now – unique and ever wiser. Should you experience the ending of a relationship, think twice and see if you can view it as an opportunity to nurture acceptance of whatever is and whatever will be. Even if you're not in a place to do this right now, someday you will be. Trust in that.

PART THREE: EMOTIONS FOR LIFE

VULNERABILITY

Interesting words and images are conjured up when we think of vulnerability; it is the state of being exposed. Society deems this state as negative, but I see it as a strength that is immensely underrated. I believe it is one of the most beautiful assets that we have. Why? For a start, it's natural; we're born with gallons of the stuff! Vulnerability shows others that we have needs to be met and elicits caring attention and gentle behaviour from others. It sends a clear, explicable message to the world that we are safe and trustworthy. Consider the wider animal kingdom. When animals want to play or communicate that they aren't a threat, they show their necks or bellies. These are vulnerable body parts, which if attacked or damaged can be fatal. Displays of this nature from our pets are declarations of trust. Now consider humankind. This wonderful innate quality facilitates meaningful and long lasting relationships, because exposure of our softer selves lets others know we are not out to compete, fight, or cause harm. Rather, we are displaying that same declaration of trust and safety, just like our cute and furry counterparts.

People inspire and connect through vulnerability. Bring to mind one of your closest relationships, someone you feel at ease with, can tell your deepest thoughts to, have experienced life's ups and downs alongside. I bet you're close with them because you've shown or shared vulnerabilities between you. I can vouch for the power of crying in front of someone for the first time, or letting that strong, exterior guard down, only to be met with compassion and kindness in the form of a knowing look, a caring smile or a safe embrace. Once this "safe zone" is reached between people, there's deeper understanding and empathy. Often it is reciprocated, forming a bond of fairness and mutual respect. The most healthy and long lasting relationships are built on foundations of real, gritty vulnerability. Over time, it becomes a less scary, more positive concept and something we see much beauty in.

Being vulnerable gives us freedom of our own emotions. It enables us to be honest to ourselves and others, showing up wholeheartedly, in all our emotional glory, with the ups, the downs and everything in between. There is no better feeling than being utterly open and raw and being accepted for just that.

Challenging the myth

Where does the greater known, negative societal myth of vulnerability come from? From a young age we are told to stand tall, to make ourselves appear bigger, to be strong. We are told not to show our weaknesses for fear of those who may prey upon us. What a sorry way to live, hiding these natural and unavoidable facets of ourselves. It uses more energy to cover up a weakness and pretend to be something we're not, but it takes more courage to raise a hand and say, "I've no idea" or "I need help". I understand that standing tall and appearing mighty may have its place and there may be times we need to do that, but for day to day life it's unnecessary, unhelpful and exhausting. Every human walking the earth knows they have weaknesses, as they have strengths. Every person understands their mortality. We have all felt afraid, exposed, embarrassed or silly. We've all failed at something, been hurt and felt judged. There is nothing bad or wrong about these feelings. They are normal and unavoidable parts of life. We just never learned to accept or manage them in our early years, because emotional intelligence was a latecomer to the curriculum and there's no manual or magic formula. Human emotions are astoundingly complex, yet this doesn't mean they need to be feared. Imagine a world where we embrace the emotional spectrum as healthy, where we view all feelings as okay, good, or dare I say – positive!

Talk about it

When our mental health is having a dip (and as we've established, we all have mental health dips) try telling someone you trust. Perhaps someone you've shown vulnerability with before, or someone you find accepting of emotions. If you're struggling to think of someone, then seek support elsewhere, from a professional, a colleague or manager. The most important thing is to talk. Let it be known. You might be surprised at the acceptance you get. You might even experience the reciprocity of your confidant opening up to you in return, sharing the load between you. I've lost count of the number of times I've heard people tell me that they never used to talk about their feelings because of the way they were brought up. Or that they never thought that mental health would affect them, until it did. What's startling is that once people begin to talk, it inspires others to do the same and one of the most powerful antidotes to mental illness is realising that we are not alone. I've experienced this too and it's an amazing catalyst for change.

Putting ourselves out there can be difficult and is almost always a little bit scary, especially when we're not feeling particularly strong. Yet stepping into this wilderness leads to new possibilities and opportunities that otherwise remain hidden. Diving into the unknown, or following a hunch can be the difference between staying stagnant and embarking on an exciting new venture. The American writer and humourist Mark Twain gleefully told us that we'll regret the things we didn't do more than the things we did do. Looking back on your life it'll surely feel better to know that you gave it a go.

Express yourself

As I mentioned earlier, that's partly why I began writing a book. Without experience or wisdom, I simply "went for it", because the thought popped into my head and I started writing about my passions, hoping that someday it would be published and make its merry way into people's palms! When I spoke about the idea at an international conference, the audience were supportive and gave me that initial boost, so I began putting chapters together right away, even though I had no idea how to become a published author. Everyone's story is worth telling and I realised that included my own. My point is, I don't see myself as an expert in the topics I write about, because what would that make me? An expert in being human, in life? That's a tall order and not one I'm comfortable to claim accountability for. I just wanted to follow an instinct and I hoped it would inspire people, because I am truly passionate about the subject and I genuinely believe we can make the world a better place by understanding and applying the good stuff.

If I'm honest (and vulnerability begins with honesty) I feel slightly vulnerable as I write this, right now. Perhaps because I'm putting pen to paper about things that are close to my heart, things I believe in. That in itself is quite exposing! Or perhaps it's because I'm acutely aware that to some people my musings may seem impractical, romantic or even foolish. Reading these chapters, you might disagree with my views, get bored and gaze beyond your page into the distant horizon. You might even judge me for the stories I tell of my life or for my opinions. There might be grammar or spelling mistakes. I'm expected to know what I'm doing because I'm a doctor and this could affect my reputation in some way. Whatever parts of ourselves we put out there in the world are open to celebration or scrutiny. How very frightening ... but I do it anyway. All because I believe that vulnerability is a human quality that is vital to living the most fulfilled life.

Still unsure? Here's something to ponder … how can vulnerability be a weakness when it takes so much strength to show it?

COURAGE

All this talk of vulnerability uncovers an important point. It resides right beside courage – the ability to do something that frightens us; strength in the face of pain or grief. Vulnerability, as we now know, is the state of being exposed. These two temperaments tend to be played against one another, as though an abundance of one means a depletion of the other. This would mean that they can't co-exist, but actually, they can, very harmoniously in fact.

Assertiveness

Courage requires assertiveness, which is defined as "confident and forceful in personality". I do wonder whether we have all this hype about assertiveness wrong and need to reframe it. Just like we have given vulnerability a bad name all this time and ought to make amends with this lovely characteristic and give it the celebration it deserves. We don't need to be forceful in order to be confident in our endeavours, or to get our needs met, or realise our wildest dreams. But we are expected to know how to get assertiveness right and that's not always easy. It can unhelpfully emerge as aggression or taking unnecessary control. My gut feeling is that we're thinking about it too much (as with a lot of things, probably!). Simply put, if we're honest in saying yes to the things we want to say yes to and saying no to the things we don't, in an open, genuine and kind way, then we are doing our best and being true to ourselves. And if we're true to ourselves, then we are being genuine.

Assertiveness is borne out of this genuine want to say yes or no; that desire for something to happen or not. It doesn't have to be hard, soft, loud or quiet. It can be all or none of those things. It is just about being true. What occurs when we are assertive in this way is that we allow others to get to know us, quirks and all. Then in turn we build deeper connections, more meaningful relationships and feel genuinely accepted by others, when we are real. It's not about being right, nor is it about winning, it isn't even about being accepted at this stage. It's merely about staying true to our values and standing up for the one person we need to take care of above all others, the one person we'll always, always need to live peacefully alongside. Our self. So trust yourself in creating the kind of life you'll be willing to live for your whole life. Then go about getting that very life, by choosing to speak your truth, openly and honestly. Your voice matters just as much as anyone else's. Being silenced is not an option.

Reflecting on what we know about connection, there are three important components: connection with others, connection with the world and connection with oneself. Being assertive with and for yourself is strengthening, enlightening and builds self esteem and confidence. It allows you to know yourself, trust yourself and stand by yourself, which I believe are vital ingredients to a happy existence. Knowing, trusting and standing by others is another effective way of acting out your values. Though it can be difficult, especially when we let our heads get involved in the decision making process of our actions and consider the consequences a little too acutely.

Of course, pausing to consider the outcome of our behaviour is a good thing, however, not at the expense of staying true to ourselves and to others who need our support. Take intimidation as an example. It happens all over the world and isn't exclusive to the school yard. We all know it's not right or nice, yet standing up for someone being harassed is something most of us would shy away from. Not because we're terrible people, but because we consider the consequences before we act. We understand that it's potentially dangerous and could cause more harm if we were to get involved. Then again, it could ease the pain and end suffering for the individual at the other end, help defuse the situation and redress the balance. It would certainly help the individual feel less alone and scared, and loneliness is something that needs combatting, for sure.

Deep down I think I've always known what the best thing to do in these situations would be, but it became clear to me the first time I read that remaining neutral in such circumstances as bullying actually assists the oppressor, never the victim. In this sense, standing aside and not getting involved when someone is struggling, means that the bully becomes stronger and worse than that, you have inadvertently supported them. The first time I realised that it made me feel a little sick to my stomach, for all the times I could have stood up and done more for a fellow human being in need. From that moment on, I spoke my mind more when I noticed a friend being talked down to, or a colleague struggling to speak up to someone in a position of authority. It doesn't always feel easy, sometimes it's downright uncomfortable, but it feels like the right thing to do and is met with gratitude from the person on the right side of the fence, every time.

Putting yourself out there for the sake of your own wellbeing is one thing. Putting yourself out there for the sake of someone else is another. Both are fulfilling and rewarding. Another nod to vulnerability then, which may be a type of assertiveness in a most beautifully unique form. It is certainly one of the most courageous ways to be.

FAILURE

What about facing the fear of failure? Knowing that you may not succeed, but giving it your best shot anyway? When I began writing a book, I didn't know the first thing about being an author when I started. It may be that people don't like what I write, the way I write and I'm almost certain there will be errors in my typing, even after several edits! I move past the fear of getting things wrong by understanding that nobody gets it all right. The misconception is that my creation had to be perfect before I let it loose into the world. That the opposite of perfect is useless. But that's not the case at all. The opposite of perfect is imperfect and that applies to everything on the planet. Look around you at the trees, plants, wildlife. Are they all the same, with identical symmetry? Perfect never arrives, the natural world isn't like that, nor does it need to be. Happy is all that matters. So, authors can hope that their readers graciously forgive the odd error or difference in opinion. The most courageous acts often stare right into the eyes of the unknown and at the very least, even if they don't go as we'd hoped, they create learning from falling.

Thinking traps

There are various thinking traps we fall into which hinder our ability to consider ourselves and what's happening around us clearly and productively. One of those traps is "black and white thinking", which is when we label an event, a person, an action or ourselves in an unnecessarily extreme sense – such as good or bad, right or wrong. Success or failure. Most of the time, events, people and behaviours are neither of these extremes but rather a mixture of both. There is a whole lot of grey between those two ends of the spectrum, yet we do like to slap a hard and fast label on things as quickly as we can. There's a neurological reason for this (as there often is!) which is to make sense of new information as effortlessly and efficiently as possible, rather than having to sit with every single new experience for long periods of time working out how to respond to it, much like a game of chess. This instantaneous labelling is based on a humungous archive of past information our brains have to hand, which has been neatly stored in the hypothetical filing cabinets of our minds, following every single experience we've lived through up until this point. The problem is that those archives have been categorised and compartmentalised via our own wonderful yet slightly warped and one-sided lens. All kinds of things are inputting to these labels, including our history, our likes and dislikes, memories, conscious and unconscious bias. The thinking trap is blindly accepting this as the full truth, without questioning it or considering alternative possibilities.

Consider this when you go through something difficult. Choosing an example that most of us are familiar with, without getting too melancholy, let's return to the example of a relationship ending. Labels get thrown around all over the place as and when we feel we need them, whether it be something they did, or the kind of person they are. Conversely, we attack ourselves and wonder why we weren't good enough or what we did that was so gravely wrong. The thinking trap here is that we are the one who is right, or we are the one who is a mess. In fact, we are rarely either of those things in totality. Others can be quick to tell us when we've made a mistake or failed them in some way and when we respect and love that person, we care about their feelings and believe what they say. Turning inwards can lead us to feel like bad people, that we are rubbish at relationships after all and should know better. Inward blaming is as damaging as outward blaming of others.

There is something calming about the notion that, in reality, the problem lies neither out there nor within you. You are neither righteous nor a mess. You just went through a break up and that's rarely plain sailing. Realising this brings about change in that you end up working on yourself a little, which is always good for personal learning and growth, yet at the same time holding a strong sense of self worth in knowing that essentially you're quite alright. If one of you pops yourself on that righteousness pedestal then there's no room for the other person to sit anywhere except on the naughty step of self loathing. We oughtn't do this to ourselves or to anyone else. As I say, in most cases, the truth tends to lie somewhere in between the two extremes. So you were never the problem, or the failure, or the mess. The bravest place to be is right in the middle.

The same goes for all those moments you previously classified as "failures". Think back and apply this same logic to every one of those events. There is always something you could have done differently, of course, there's always more we can do. Simultaneously, perhaps it was always going to happen that way because of some other reasons way beyond your control. The magic lies in accepting both realities.

Failure is learning

Laura Gassner Otting (2020) is known as a "confidence catalyst" and urges us to see failure as fulcrum, rather than final. She uses an analogy of walking along a route and reaching what appears to be the end of the road, at which point we are free to wonder, "does the road end here for me or do I just need to learn how to hike now?" Perhaps the road becomes an overgrown path for a while, but with the right equipment we can keep going. If we reach a roadblock, while we may stumble and scratch our heads for a moment, eventually we'll climb, crawl, dig or curve our way around it. We might build a vehicle to get us over it. We might enlist some help from others to heave us over. If there really is no way around the roadblock, then we find another route to travel instead. So seeing failure as fulcrum means that this is the point at which something happens to create a change in energy and effort, a different way of thinking or seeing the situation. Essentially, moments of perceived failure are our best opportunities to learn.

Imagine how you would feel and behave if failure were impossible. Next time you want to try something new or reach towards a goal, act as though failure doesn't exist (safely, I might add) and see where it takes you. What a way to live life!

Perhaps failures are in fact delayed achievements.

CELEBRATING THE "NEGATIVES"

Exploring my own failures, achievements and the courage it took to go for them, led me to consider the concept of negative emotions and how we might celebrate these too. Take regret, which many people are resistant to admit into their lives, as though it comes with a fatal disease. Feelings and emotions associated with regret include guilt, shame, sadness, disappointment, self blame and frustration. None of which we relish. However, these are incredible emotions that are indicating important messages or lessons upon which we can build a fulfilled life, should we have the courage to tune in to them and listen. We may not have succeeded the first time around but there's nothing to stop us succeeding in the future. Regret encourages us to act differently next time, so I don't see it as a bad emotion that must be avoided, rather it's a beacon towards a better path. Feeling regretful means that I won't travel the same road again, it makes me want to do all I can to make the most of the here and now, to not waste time on difficulties and to resolve upsets as quickly as possible. I regret not asking a loved one more about the meaningful things before they passed away. It doesn't make me despise myself, nor does it make me a bad person. It does however make me think more about the people I have in my life and spending more meaningful time with them, rather than focusing on inane things that are trivial, repetitive and quite frankly, pointless.

A story about regret

The best thing about embracing regret is that it enables us to take notice of the important aspects of life that we might otherwise neglect, while there's still time to do something about it. That wasn't the case for one of my own regrets and whilst not ideal, it has taught me an important lesson about what to do next time I'm met with this uncomfortable emotion.

My first serious and long term boyfriend was someone I adored for years in my early twenties. We were young and in love. I'd known nothing like it and our connection was deep. The wise amongst us know that adoration and love don't necessarily equate to being right and this was the case for the two of us. The paths that my boyfriend and I would take were to be separate; we weren't destined for a lifetime together, however much of a wrench that felt at the time. We thought a lot of each other, shared many experiences, explored and had fun, got lost and found, felt the intensity of feelings that were previously unrivalled. In some ways, that kind of innocent love would never be replicated, because we went through many hardships for the first time together and never stopped adoring one another. Inevitably, we went our separate ways. For a time, we tried to be friends, but that was proving difficult so I thought it best to have little contact. I behaved in accordance with what I felt was right and I accept my decision as I made it with all the best intentions and the resources I had at my disposal at that time. Little did I know that I would later experience regret.

One of my lifelong best friends was calling on my phone. Excitedly, I answered. We always had so much to talk about and over the years, our friendship was strong. I was in my bedroom at the time and saw myself in the mirror as her tone of voice told me that this wasn't a friendly catch up call. My facial expression dropped and I sat on the edge of the bed, as she trembled the words, "he's been in a plane crash." I couldn't believe what I was hearing. Sheer disbelief. This good man who worked hard, loved his family and was popular amongst our friends, who was strong and soft at the same time, who I'd spent so many loving moments with, was missing along with the others on that flight. In the days that followed, I kept up with as much news as I could about the search for the plane that had gone missing in the mountains. We hoped it had merely flown off the radar, or had landed somewhere that passengers could be rescued by those tirelessly searching for them. Finally, the unwanted news came. No survivors. Fragments of the aircraft and the people who so tragically lost their lives were identified. It was unimaginable, horrific, yet happening. He had his life ahead of him and his family will never fill the hole in their hearts. Suddenly, this person I shared so many memories with was gone. The years we shared were only mine to remember. Grief and sadness came first, with a heavy heart for those who were closest to him. Regret descended when I realised that I'd never told him, when our hearts had healed, that I thought of him with only fondness. It sat uncomfortably with me that I couldn't tell him now, that he'd never know; it was out of my control. It may remain one of my regrets and I've come to understand that's okay. I don't fight against it because it was a lesson, a tough but valuable one.

You see, we simply never know what's around the next corner or how we're going to feel about it. There are countless external factors that we have no control over, some grossly unexpected and tragic eventualities. We can't possibly plan for them all. We make choices based on our emotions and every action has a consequence, sometimes favourable, sometimes not. It's a big responsibility and at the same time, there isn't much we can do about it. We can't see into the future and that would be the only way to truly avoid regret. The only thing we can do, is embrace this feeling and grow from it.

Nowadays, I try my best to let people know what they mean to me and resolve misunderstandings or upsets with as much communication and honesty, as quickly as possible. Too often we wait, we wonder, we deliberate and end up doing nothing. Too often we don't let others know how special they are and what an impact they've had on us. Whereas I may once have seen it as silly, unnecessary or inappropriate, I now see it as a courageous act of kindness to open my heart and tell someone what I really think.

Reframing "bad feelings"

I'm really not sure why regret has been tainted with such a bad reputation. Perhaps because it's an uncomfortable emotion that we shy away from, a little like guilt and shame. I want to relieve this emotion of its negative connotations and free it up to play a positive role in our lives. There are no "bad" emotions unless you've fallen into the black and white thinking trap. Go ahead and have the odd regret. Let them teach you great things. Don't let them fester, nor become your focus for long, but do let them be what they are and let them be your guide to becoming an even better version of you. Regrets can help you make some wonderful changes in your life and bring you closer to people (not to mention closer to yourself) in magical ways. If there's someone in your life who doesn't know how amazing they are, tell them. Get a message to them now. You're much less likely to regret doing that, than never getting around to it.

Guilt and shame

It's impossible for me to explore deeply the concepts of failure and regret without stumbling clumsily across a couple of emotions that most of us would probably erase if we had such superpowers to do so: guilt and shame. You have the measure of me by now; this is my attempt to reframe all the experiences that humans are simply going to go through at some stage in their existence. You know the ones, those feelings we have to sit alongside yet can't seem to get comfortable and cosy up with. I hope we can begin to find peace with them, by understanding, being aware, being honest, raw and real. And by accepting it all. So let's dive in (gingerly, of course. I'm open water certified which means there are depths that I'm yet to learn to reach, but we can enjoy going as far as we can with the skills we have).

Guilt is an emotional experience of remorse or responsibility in response to your own actions that have violated some moral code of conduct in some way. Some describe it as an intense worry. It's associated with the feeling of wrongdoing towards another. Shame is directed inwards, bringing with it a raft of other experiences such as foolishness, dishonour, humiliation, ridicule, loss of respect or self esteem. Both guilt and shame can feel unpleasant. They are used interchangeably but, put simply, guilt refers to how you feel about others and shame refers to how you feel about yourself.

Both guilt and shame are purposeful and can teach us about our values, behaviours and how we want to grow as we navigate through life. Somehow, we need to accept guilt and shame as helpful guides alongside failure (I know, this is getting tough now but we can do this!). To make a good start, we simply express these feelings and tell our stories. Keeping shame to ourselves gives it the power to render us alone with the belief that nobody else will understand or love us. It takes courage and vulnerability to express shame, which we now know are strengths. Reaching out to others when we feel guilt or shame helps generate empathy from those who are ready to hear and understand. Choose wisely and begin by sharing your stories with people you trust to care about you. When they give you a different perspective of your narrative, it can alleviate the pain of these feelings and help you to understand why you did what you did, or feel the way you feel.

It's not about others eliminating our painful feelings for us, it's about recognising that we're human; it's validating. It's important that the recipients of our stories are empathic rather than judgemental. With judgement, shame can elicit anger and this, in turn, damages relationships with disrespect, distrust and betrayal. If this happens and you become aware of it, all is not lost. Love can survive this damage as long as it is acknowledged, healed and doused with kindness, affection and mutual understanding. When dealt with empathically, the sharing of guilt and shame can be one of the most powerful foundations for deep and meaningful relationships. Having someone who is able to sit alongside our shame, someone who recognises their own shame well enough to handle both, to see one another's shame and love each other because of it, is a truly special gift.

All emotions are okay

To live wholeheartedly, we must embrace the feelings of not being good enough, of not being worth it, especially when these feelings are so intense that we're afraid to stop long enough to feel them. Allow them in and allow them to have their time, that way they'll do what they need to do, teach you want you need to be taught, then they'll pass. It would be ridiculous to think that our species were built with capacities for feelings that have no protective function whatsoever. Remember, we are animals and at the end of the day, we have evolved to survive. Everything we feel has a reason and tapping into these reasons helps us accept them for what they are. Humans also have the capacity to think about their emotions, which other animals don't possess. It's a treat that we can think ourselves into a better frame of mind. It's all about gaining perspective and taking small steps to move forwards. No emotions are bad and no emotions last forever. The bravest thing of all is to welcome the lot with your arms wide open.

AUTHENTICITY

Oscar Wilde suggested, "Be yourself. Everyone else is taken." It's funny how simple this advice is yet how many times we stop ourselves from following it. Be truly you, no matter what. If you're feeling fantastic, then show it. Nervous? Admit it. Passionate about something? Express it. As low as you've ever felt in your entire life? Share it. There are people navigating dark moments, believing the delusional societal norm that everyone else is coping better and that they mustn't get "too emotional" or behave in "extreme ways" or heaven forbid, cry in public. Show me a human being who's never cried, never shouted in distress, never become angry, never felt like giving up. We've all been children after all, right? We've all experienced the wonderful range of colourful emotions before, naturally, right from birth. Then we get a little older and we're taught to hide them, control them, repress them. What shame this brings to us. What shame and what a shame. The fact is, this rainbow of emotion doesn't simply disappear because societal constraints leave us feeling bad about having them. There are lots of perfectly reasonable ways we can express our feelings appropriately and honestly. When we do, people see us, because we've shown up in the world as ourselves. That's authenticity. The reciprocal effect is that others take this as permission to do the same and people are grateful to have the opportunity to be open and honest. To feel safe in being vulnerable. To be human.

The first time I saw the Pixar film Inside Out I was taken aback by the profound message in a children's animation. Through the experiences of a little girl Riley, it shows us what people can gain from allowing sadness in and how constantly trying to override sadness with joy doesn't help us through difficulties. What is this telling those young people watching? That negative emotions are just as vital as positive emotions. That all emotions are real, genuine and emerge for good reason. That all emotions need to be given attention and space. This is how we reach a state of balance, calm, contentedness, or what I like to call "happiness". Almost a century before this lovely Pixar animation, American poet and playwright E. E. Cummings put a similar message out into the world when he said, "it takes courage to grow up and become who you really are."

When are we going to start listening to these inspirational characters? How about now? When you're struggling, don't hide away, don't keep a lid on things, don't feel ashamed or worried about what judgements you might receive. Those who judge are simply scared of those emotions themselves, because they never had permission to let them out either. Or perhaps they're so focused on reassuring themselves that they just don't have the energy or skillset to reassure you too. Give the greatest gift to them and to yourself by permitting it, all of it! By letting the world have some of your wonderful, open, truthful emotion. Let others in. Let yourself out. Be right there. Be you. Be seen. Be bright.

Embrace who you are

Brené Brown (2010) defines authenticity as "the daily practice of letting go of who we think we're supposed to be and embracing who we actually are." I'm still in the process of building the courage to do this more and more and it's scary at times. But when I see others embracing their feelings, their strengths and their personalities, I look up to them as people who are living their lives to the full. Seemingly unafraid. Inspiring and impressive. I see it and I want it. As we've established, the decision about my own behaviour is mine and it's up to me and only me to make that happen for myself. To live my life in that fantastic way. Allow me to return to the idea of unadulterated passionate expression for a moment and recall a magical memory ...

A little while ago I posted a video onto my social media channels of a man playing the piano at St Pancras train station in London. Picture the scene. His bike was resting next to the piano and his work bag was still on his back. He'd stopped briefly during a work shift to play. He played Beethoven's Moonlight Sonata in an incredibly unique fashion, improvising wonderfully with his own tilt on the music. After a few moments of listening, I realised he was beatboxing at the same time, adding another layer of himself to the well known classical piece. He threw himself dramatically around on the piano stool, as if he and the music were completely connected. The music moved him and he moved the music. I dare say that most of us would avoid doing something like this for sheer fear of judgement and utter embarrassment. But nobody thought he looked like a fool that day.

Crowds gathered and watched in awe at this man, who none of us knew, who was simply expressing himself wildly in public. Everyone loved it. Strangers smiled at strangers. That video post got tens of thousands of views and an abundance of lovely comments about self expression, courage, showing up in the world and being ourselves. We enjoy it, we want it, so let's do it, for ourselves and for others! One of your first thoughts in a situation like that might be, "But what if I make a mistake, fail or look silly?" Elizabeth Lesser, co-founder of the largest health focused education centre in the USA, rightfully pointed out that all human beings, including the Dalai Lama (possibly the most peaceful meditator on the planet), make mistakes. They all have anxieties, fears and worries. Nobody has it all perfectly sorted. The aim then isn't to become perfect but to become authentic. Let this be your mantra.

Be honest

Remember the last first date you had? Wasn't there at least a part of you trying to be the very best version of yourself, smiling more than usual, letting little annoyances go and making sure you didn't allow certain parts of yourself (those bits you don't like) show? The reason being, to make sure they like you enough to want to see you again. How about your last job interview? Remember sitting up straight, articulating your words as correctly as possible and producing the best verbal answers you could possibly muster, probably feeling utterly exhausted afterwards for the mere fact that all your energy was taken up thinking of big words and impressive examples of when you perfectly dealt with conflict. It's common to try to present ourselves in the best possible light for people we perceive to have some authority in deciding whether or not we're a good candidate – for the job or for the role of partner. This is okay to an extent, in certain circumstances. But wouldn't it be easier and simpler if nobody did that? We could all relax fully into ourselves and just be open and honest from the start. No judgement, no anxiety around not being chosen, less competition with the next person in line being similarly selective about how they present themselves.

I'd love to live in a world where we're honest, right from the outset. About lots of things, particularly who we are and how we feel. Being honest is a form of kindness. It allows others to really see into our souls. It gives them the choice to really know us and decide whether we're a good fit. Surely that's better in the long run? Perhaps we'd save ourselves a lot of time and energy. Being authentic prompts others to do the same, by having real conversations. It's liberating and puts us all on a more equal footing.

Your contract with life

We don't get to choose everything that happens to us. Trying to avoid being disliked, judged or misunderstood is like trying to avoid breathing in air. It's going to happen, unless we cut our interactions with anyone or anything down to zero. Some events help us, other events hinder us. Some people help us, other people hinder us. The best we can do is accept it all as part of the reality of life. There will be ups and downs and we can't have it all our way, fabulous as that would be! Tough times and the emotions that follow are all part of our contract with life. We get the good and the bad. That's the deal. So many people say they don't want to feel negative emotions, avoid anything that makes them feel afraid, upset, lost or hurt, or that they daren't try because they might be disappointed or make a fool of themselves. This is understandable of course, but as Susan David (psychologist and author who coined the term "emotional agility") put it, "these are dead people's goals" (David, 2016). It's good to let go of those events and people who hinder us, to the point where they're not a part of our everyday worlds, yet remain conscious of their existence, because we've learned valuable lessons from the way they touched our souls.

Strong and soft

Coupling our new favourite emotion – vulnerability – with courage, means that we can feel strong in our core values, stand up for what we believe in and be true to ourselves, whilst simultaneously offering a kind and caring energy. The outside world receives us as soft and strong, all at the same time, in the very best of ways. Joan Halifax (Buddhist teacher and founder of the Upaya Institute and Zen Centre) conceptualised this as having a strong back and a soft front (Halifax, 2011). It's not always easy, especially when we've been hurt or wronged. In these times, our fronts become hardened because we want to protect ourselves with hypothetical armour. We want to make sure we build big enough walls or create bold enough boundaries so that others won't hurt or wrong us in the same ways. So we dial up the courage and the hard back, whilst dialling down the vulnerability and the soft front. In theory, I get it, but in reality, it rarely works. If it does work, it's at the expense of something magnificent which is depth of feeling, meaningful relationships and passionate experiences. Vulnerability becomes the enemy, which it most definitely is not. Vulnerability is where many of our most precious emotions emerge, including love, joy, intimacy and trust.

Nurturing a soft front is actually one of the most courageous acts. Giving up on vulnerability lets negativity and hardship win. Let's not do that. I love the metaphor of a "strong back and soft front" which means we can show our squishy sides whilst maintaining integrity with a powerful core. The image of standing proudly whilst opening up about your true feelings comes to mind. We can bring our hearts into the arena so that they offer intuitive wisdom to our heads. Our hearts are the playful, curious and wild parts of us and allow us to bring love, kindness and fear alongside robustness and bravery. These elements of us are exquisitely compatible; we can be all these things at once in a beautiful mix of tough and tender. This aligns nicely with my earlier point on acceptance, in that we are complex and changeable, do not fit neatly into one box all the time, and that's okay. I dare say that having a wild heart would call for it.

Emotional freedom

In short, it's about being real, honest and genuine. This might seem simple or obvious, but more often than we'd like, we put on a show and behave in ways that are not quite in line with how we really feel. This doesn't make us cheats or liars or bad people. It just means we've learned to live in a world of expectations, social norms, stigma and consequences. My hope is that we can be more authentic about our mental health, break down barriers and be true to ourselves and others. We can begin right now in being role models in showing others that it's okay to be ourselves, it's okay to be different and it's okay to not be okay sometimes too.

Let me tell you more about that personal story I reflected on by the water that day, to better illustrate some of my musings about how very essential vulnerability and authenticity are ...

About a year before I began writing my book was the peak point of that particularly difficult phase, whereby I experienced a relationship breakdown, a redundancy, a house move and a deterioration in health. All at the same time. It hit me hard. So hard that I didn't believe I could live through it. I wasn't sure I wanted to. If I could've made an easy decision to leave this earth calmly and not upset my loved ones in the process, I'd have taken it. No question. I remember hearing someone say, "I don't want to die, I just don't want to live either" and thinking, "Yes, I get that."

The hardest blow was when I was told by a loved one (the other person in that relationship breakdown) that my emotions weren't okay. I felt silenced and stonewalled, that I shouldn't need to talk or seek support because adults ought to stand on their own two feet. I didn't realise how damaging this could be, until I was knee deep in despising myself for it. The worst thing about it was the subtlety. Onlookers would never have guessed. It wasn't obvious, there was no aggression or physical evidence, yet the psychological upheaval shook my foundations. Over time, my opinions and ways of being were called into question. I learned to tolerate and not rock the boat, for fear of the upset it could cause. I was told what the behaviour of "good people" looked like and most of the time, this didn't match mine, therefore I couldn't help but feel inherently bad. Having a difference of opinion became deeply uncomfortable and I gradually began to change to fit into his ideal, because I had come to believe it was better. But it wasn't. My honest thoughts were dismissed, my natural actions were judged and my real emotions were deemed wrong. I was moulding into someone I wasn't and being myself no longer felt like an option. I felt a power imbalance, which meant it took a while before I saw that he was projecting his own struggles onto me.

His behaviour caused me to feel awfully alone and like a bad person. His disengagement from my true nature triggered fear and shame of being abandoned and unlovable. And when there's no specific event to point to, it can make you feel crazy. Attempts to explain his impact on me were met with grave reactions, so I didn't even dare name it. I tried to hide my emotions and not let them show in case others judged me too. The easiest way to describe it is that I had to tone down who I was. Things I felt passionate, excited, scared or angry about were muted, so as not to cause issue or offence. At first I found it unusual, then tiring and eventually oppressive. A slow process I didn't see happening until I was out the other side and people named it for me. Essentially, I stopped being authentically me. I didn't want to have to endure any more of anything, because none of it made sense. I was struggling with so much and the person who promised to keep me safe was doing the opposite. That was the lowest point in my life. I simply wanted it to be over.

Luckily, my caring family and friends asked how I was, and asked again, until I eventually felt able to open up and express myself honestly again. They empathised that I was going through a lot and allowed me to feel what I felt, without judgement or criticism; a concept called psychological safety. They pointed out to me that feeling so confused and like a bad person were merely symptoms of this relationship and that deep down I knew the truth. Gradually, I realised that my emotions weren't too much, in fact, they were normal, people understood and opened up about how they too had felt the same when their lives had taken some twists and turns that tested them. I was just another human being grappling with that contract with life. I wasn't feeling anything that a million other people hasn't felt before me. I wasn't alone. I was okay. It was normal. What a revelation, what a relief. This may well have saved my life.

Once I had trusted humankind and allowed myself to get back to being vulnerable and authentic, the weight quickly lifted. I didn't need a diagnosis or label, nor did I seek them, because deep down I already knew it was all a normal part of living and it isn't always easy. I didn't need easy. What I needed was acceptance, understanding, hope, patience, support, kindness and of course, time. By allowing myself to be me, I didn't have to pretend, or hide my feelings, or be someone I wasn't. We are allowed to feel whatever we feel and that's the liberty of emotional freedom. Finally, all those parts of my life – work, home, health and love – grew better and stronger again.

Whilst this was a horrific experience, I don't harbour any grudges towards another human being. I feel for the person who wronged me, because I choose to believe it wasn't his intention and that he couldn't help it. With respect to him, I don't even think he realised it. Some people unintentionally cause harm and it doesn't make them evil. It does, however, mean that we must be certain in ourselves when we get that gut feeling that someone is disallowing us to be who we are. I didn't know how to do this at the time but I've since learned a lot about relationships, in particular, how to trust yourself alongside someone else, enabling dependence and maintaining emotional freedom. Let's explore this a little.

From turmoil to trust

Trust is a willingness to be vulnerable based on the expectations of others. All relationships have a degree of dependency and expectation, which serves as a solid foundation for the future. We can join with another person without losing ourselves.

Belgian psychotherapist Esther Perel (2020) explains how we are raised for loyalty or autonomy. A loyalty base means that we turn to others when we encounter problems, because we know that they are able and willing to help. An autonomy base means that we attempt to fix problems by ourselves, believing we have the answers. I see value in each, but I prefer loyalty because it breeds community, mutual dependence and trust and I am reassured to hear it. Recognise when you and your partner are coming from different bases and decide whether you're okay with that, whether you can meet in the middle or whether you can't.

Practise checking in with your heart, as well as your head. If your heart is okay with the situation, then it's probably alright. If your heart is sending you an alarm message, listen and let it tell you why.

Know that one person's opinion of you doesn't make them right. They don't get to tell you how to be. Nobody holds absolute truth, only their perspective which is coloured by their own history, experiences and pain. We all have biases (often subconscious) and nobody has it all figured out. Accepting this of ourselves and others is revolutionary. Hurtful behaviour is often guided by fear and knowing this allows us to forgive. We can't be held accountable for being the person in turmoil as well as accountable for the person who's unable to cope with the turmoil. That's illogical. People who are peaceful inside can handle others' distress. Someone's inability to be by your side, no matter which parts of yourself are on show, isn't your fault. It simply signals you to look elsewhere for support and give them compassion to find their own. The power of this is when anger and despair are replaced with empathy and gratitude. Whoever said that hindsight is a wonderful thing was a wise person indeed.

If you're constraining your behaviours or opinions for fear of upsetting someone, ask yourself what's right. Tap into that inner compass and be guided by your unique set of values, then you won't go far wrong. Move towards people you don't need to edit yourself around. Sometimes, no matter how nice you try to be, whatever olive branch you offer, however many resolutions you attempt, others won't meet you there. That's their choice. No matter how unfair, don't let their resistance to positivity become yours. Remember that you have a finite amount of time and energy to spend here, so surround yourself with people who let you be, who let you shine as you. It's an honour that engenders compassion, empathy, love and understanding of diversity.

Then there's forgiveness. Making peace with these experiences is liberating. For a long while, I carried around someone else's disturbances, because he projected them onto me. As a psychologist, you'd think I'd have seen that coming. We're all human; I keep returning to this. To forgive, it helps to have a tangible ending, which can take many forms. For me, it was a note of acceptance. I explicitly forgave and reached out to the good part of him, still believing that we all have goodness inside. Of course, he dismissed it and had one last attempt at making me feel small. The difference was, I'd moved to a place where he couldn't touch me anymore. I trusted myself, had control over myself and I gave all his control back to him. I had grown and didn't absorb his anguish. Psychologically, I left it all where it belonged – with him. That was my ending and the best part is, he needn't ever know. So engage in whatever ending ritual works for you. All that matters is how it makes you feel and that you stand by your good self.

You can be everything

I'll never be the same after that tricky time, nor would I want to be. Don't get me wrong, I love being descried as an "up person", an optimist, fun, radiating positivity. But my revelation was that I also love being raw and real and sometimes that means I'm a little down and not so fun. These are two sides of the same coin and do not have to be mutually exclusive. We can live well and be both up and down at different times. It's all about how open we are to being vulnerable and authentic, how we understand our feelings, how we accept them for what they are and how we move forwards through difficult times. Life is full to the brim with lessons and these lessons beat us over the head until we learn from them, then they go along their merry way having left their legacy with us. Our experiences and lessons change us for the better, when we allow them to. So change is good, because it means we've developed and grown following an event that held significant meaning for us. To quote Charlie Chaplin, "I found that anguish and emotional suffering are only warning signs that I was living my own truth. Today I know this as authenticity."

So what if we get things wrong? It's plain to see that if you live truly and show up as yourself no matter what, then every decision you ever made, no matter where it leads, was the right decision for you at that time in your life. If you made those decisions with a whole heart, then your life would never have gone any other way and you did the best you could. There's an incredible peace in looking back over your years and knowing that.

If I gave you just one piece of advice today, it would be this – do whatever you do wholeheartedly and authentically. If you do that and nothing else, then at the very least you'll be living a life that's true to yourself and attract people and opportunities that are in line with who you are. What else could you possibly need?

CERTAINTIES

People like the feeling of certainty, that they know what's going on and understand why things are happening. You might go so far as to admit that you like to be in control. There's nothing wrong with that, except the fact that you're only in control of yourself, nothing else. One of the greatest mental reliefs is to accept that uncertainty is okay.

There are very few guarantees in life. We can depend on two things happening. One being the inevitable event of death. I used to be afraid of dying, the thought of not being here anymore was more than I could bear. If I thought about it too much, I had to distract myself in order to intercept the uncomfortable physiological response at the mere thought of such a final and irreversible eventuality. Perhaps the most extreme form of FOMO (fear of missing out) because I was enjoying experiencing all that life had to offer and I didn't want the fun to stop. I loved life so much that I couldn't stomach the thought of no longer having it. I'd been so fortunate growing up, saw myself as lucky, was hopeful and optimistic about my future and apart from the usual setbacks, didn't really have too much to worry about. I was having a great time. I was loving being alive. In my thirties, the difficult events I described earlier, the ones that I hadn't anticipated let alone planned for, those that I would never have chosen to go through, occurred in quick succession. One by one they pushed me to my limits, eventually right to my own edge.

My coping mechanisms were tested, my resilience stretched, my heart and soul were chipped away at and most of the things I'd always believed in were called into question at some point during those years. I stopped describing life as fun. I didn't love it anymore. I found it a chore. I found the very act of living hard.

It wasn't a sudden realisation but over time, dying didn't seem so bad anymore. I never thought I'd act on these feelings and certainly had no plans to do so, but I certainly stopped fearing the end of my life, because it seemed it could be easier not to have to deal with it all. They say that everything happens for a reason. Maybe that's why all my buttons were pushed and why I was taken to my outer limits and my own edge – to cure my fear of death. A silver lining even around the greyest cloud.

There's a potential positive outcome that comes from contemplating death. If someone told you that these moments right now will be among your last, how would you spend them? Would you behave differently, smile more, do more good things for others, slow down and enjoy the ride? We are all going to die (that's the certainty) we just don't know when. Oughtn't we live in such a way that it wouldn't make a difference when that fate came? Say what needs to be said, do what needs to be done, be fully present in the moment without fear of what happens next. Michael Singer (author and founder of a meditation centre) proposes that your interaction with life is your most meaningful relationship (Singer, 2007). Instead of being afraid of death, see it as your educator and learn what it has to teach you about life. He believes that death doesn't take away, but gives meaning to everything you have and all you do, while it waits patiently for as long as it can so that you can live your best life in the meantime.

The second guarantee in life is that nothing stays the same. Whatever you're going through right now, whatever is happening to you or around you, won't stay the same forever.

Everything changes, to a greater or lesser degree. Knowing that whatever difficult feelings and emotions you're currently experiencing will eventually pass, can offer great comfort. Our new friend death has made a promise to us that "this too shall pass".

With these two guarantees in mind, we gain an alternative and healthier standpoint on many things. By contemplating our mortality and knowing that everything changes, we can learn to bend and flex with life's challenges, accept changes and make the most of all we have, while we have it, with gratitude every small step of the way.

HAPPY BRAIN, HAPPY BODY

People who haven't yet experienced the gravity and power behind vulnerability and authenticity may view them as a little "soft and fluffy". There's nothing soft nor fluffy about finding the sheer strength and courage to bare your innermost thoughts and feelings for the sake of being real. Having said that, as a scientist in the field of mind and behaviour, I understand the need for the scientific edge, which is why I've peppered my thoughts and suggestions with research based evidence. Let's bring out the neuro-geek within us and talk about that three pounds of fat and grey matter that we carry around in our heads every day.

The brain is the most complex organ in the human body and houses about as many neurons as there are stars in the Milky Way (approximately 80–100 billion). These neurons are connected by synapses and transmit information via electrical impulses throughout the brain and body; some scientists say this happens at speeds of up to 250 mph (Nature Editorial, 2018). Contrary to popular belief, we use most parts of our brain in any given day and it remains at least partially active all of the time.

Our brains need us to help keep them fit and healthy, just as our bodies do. Every minute, up to a litre of blood flows through your brain, carrying a constant supply of oxygen. It may surprise you to learn that the harder you think, the more oxygen your brain uses from your bloodstream. Another reason to let go of those racing thoughts and give your brain (and blood supply) a breather now and again. In a waking state, your brain generates up to 25 watts of power, which may be why we use the metaphor of a lightbulb to denote a new idea!

Don't believe all you think

I have a few questions for you to ponder, momentarily. Do you believe everything you read? Do you believe everything others tell you? How about all that you see in the media? Then why do you believe everything you tell yourself? Our brains are fantastically intelligent yet simultaneously impressionable. We seem to genuinely believe all we tell ourselves, good, bad and indifferent. This can go terribly wrong, especially with incessant negative self chatter. But unless we truly think of ourselves as the single, most knowledgeable, enlightened, self aware, intellectual being that ever walked the earth, then surely some of that self chatter can be misguided, right?

Remember, the average human has thousands of thoughts in any given day, which are often largely negative and repetitive. Let's pause on that for a moment – the vast majority of the things you've thought about today are the same things you thought about yesterday and are doing your mental health a disservice because, for the most part, they're not even nice. Imagine how light our lives would be if we freed up some of that brain space for novel and happy cognitions. Or calming insights. Or sheer nothingness. A vacation for our heavy hemispheres may just be the ticket to serenity. Our bodies benefit from a break from active strain, when we sit down to relax or when we lie down to sleep. We ought to allow our minds the same down time. And often. Simply being aware of and not believing every single thought that dashes into our consciousness is a very good first step indeed. The next step is to get out of that constant rush of thinking and let a lot of it go. It's time to learn new cognitive habits.

What a brain!

There are different brain areas that are responsible for different functions and neuroscientists offer many explanations. Understanding our brains can be mind boggling (ironically). One way of looking at this astonishing organ nestled snugly inside our skulls is that it is broadly comprised of three functional components, as physician and neuroscientist Paul MacLean (1990) put it, the reptilian, emotional and thinking brain.

The reptilian brain is deep within the core and is the most ancient. Responsible for primitive drives such as regulating body temperature, thirst, hunger, blood glucose levels, sex drive and releasing hormones essential to everyday tasks, it keeps us in balance.

The emotional brain lies beneath the cerebral cortex and emerged evolutionarily in mammals. Within this mammalian brain are the amygdala (which responds quickly and automatically to perceived threats in our environments) and the hypothalamus (which regulates the fight, flight freeze response), which are just two of the many structures within the complex limbic system. They are involved in the innate survival mechanisms and responsive behaviours occur without conscious thought; they are automatic. This is great when we need to preserve our life, because we don't need to waste time or energy on considering the pros and cons of punching a bear on the nose or running for the hills! By this point, the bear has undoubtedly won the game so it's a no brainer (pardon the pun) that we hand over to our sympathetic nervous system in times of serious danger. The limbic system is also responsible for activating the parasympathetic nervous system, which is a state of physiological calm during periods of low energy, such as when we need to rest or digest and when our environment is safe.

The thinking brain is the neocortex (the logical, reasoning

centres) and is most developed in primates, especially humans who have the largest prefrontal cortex of all animals. In times of stress, the emotional brain bursts into action first, releasing chemicals such as cortisol and adrenaline through the adrenal glands and into the nervous system (the electrical wiring of your whole body). Whilst this is happening automatically, our thinking brain can be brought in to help make sense of the situation and calm us down, de-activating the sympathetic nervous system and activating the parasympathetic nervous system, introducing calming chemicals such as acetylcholine, making us feel better.

So how do we leverage the skills of our emotional and thinking brains to serve us well? First, we need to be aware of what's happening, then we need to understand what we can do about it.

Emotions are signals to inform us that something is occurring which we need to be aware of and respond to. Our brains release different hormones depending on our immediate experiences and environments, in order to get us moving in a direction towards helping ourselves, whether that be preserving our lives by moving away from danger or towards something good for us. Our human superpower is that we can choose how we feel, which other animals can't do. We have the luxury of a large prefrontal cortex, giving us the capacity to think situations through so that we can problem solve, consider options and choose our responses based on which emotions are most appropriate.

In order to be the best version of yourself, your brain can be your most prized asset and best friend. To set the wheels of success in motion, begin with a brief check in with yourself every day, ideally in the morning and later on during the day too. Ask yourself two simple questions, "How am I feeling?" and "What do I need?" Give yourself a numeric score between 1 and 10 on the hypothetical mental wellbeing scale if it helps to keep tabs on how you're doing. As long as you monitor your own wellbeing daily, you'll have a greater sense of your overall wellbeing, whether it's on its way up or down and what you need to do about it in order to stay in tip top condition as much as possible. If you find yourself sliding down the wellbeing scale, it's time to explore your options. Generate a toolkit so that you've got enough in your armour to draw upon during times of need.

Get a stress toolkit

Emiliya Zhivotovskaya (founder of The Flourishing Centre) tells us that we can use various in the moment physical and mental techniques to reduce the build up of stress hormones in our brains and bodies (Zhivotovskaya, 2020). But how do you decide whether it's a physical or mental tool that you need?

We must tune in with our instinct and not allow our minds to cloud our otherwise well-placed judgement. Often, we have an intuitive drive towards something (some people call this a gut feeling), then rapidly attempt to process this through the lens of cognitive reasoning, rationality, or analytical thinking. These executive functioning skills are innate in humans, with their hefty frontal lobes. They work wonders when we need to weigh up the pros and cons of an idea, forecast scenarios based on a myriad of data, or some other complex task that requires careful consideration. Some circumstances however don't call for such deep thought processes, in fact, over thinking can simply get in the way of what we intuitively know to be right.

Trust yourself and stop questioning yourself to the point of utter confusion, or worse still, to the point of a non-decision because it all became too complicated. Most things in life aren't complicated at all, if we follow our hearts (aka gut, intuition, instinct, third eye chakra – take your pick. It doesn't matter what you call it, as long as you attend to it). Let's get back to our self check in questions. Once you've got into the habit of asking yourself how you're feeling and what you need, you'll become well-versed in making on the spot decisions about whether it's a physical or mental technique that you need to dig out of that wellbeing toolbox. Like any other health habit, this takes a little effort at first but within a few weeks or so, it becomes second nature and you'll notice the benefits fairly quickly, as long as you're choosing something that works for you and tuning in to your mind and body. Your mind and your body both belong to you and only you, so take notice of them and look after them. You only get one of each.

Physical tools

By learning how to leverage our breath, we can take some control of our own nervous system. Each inhalation stimulates the sympathetic (activating) nervous system and each exhalation stimulates the parasympathetic (relaxing) nervous system. If you're prone to anxiety, you may be inhaling longer than you're exhaling through life. By taking slower, more controlled, deep belly breaths and exhaling for longer than we inhale, we calm ourselves physiologically by activating the parasympathetic nervous system and decreasing the stress hormones and reducing our heart rates, simultaneously.

Our largest sense organ is our skin. Touch is related to trust, which are both associated with increased oxytocin. Appropriate touch helps alleviate stress. Choose comfy clothes, have a bath or shower, grab a hug, engage in psychosensory therapy which includes self massage or relaxing your tense muscles. As if you need any more reason, engaging in these types of touch elicit a delta brain wave frequency which is associated with good sleep.

Have you ever wondered why people enjoy singing so much? Singing causes the vagus nerve (as it passes through our neck) to vibrate and this nerve is the calming nerve that runs through the whole body. So turn the music up, join a choir or sing in the street.

What about having a good cry? Researchers have found that we release cortisol in our tears, so if we have too much of this particular stress hormone pumping around and we feel that need for a fast release, then a good weep can do the trick!

The list of physical tools for engendering pleasant emotions is endless, just so long as you're treating yourself well, being kind to yourself and engaging all your senses, you'll be on your way to finding what works for you.

Mental tools

Certain situations call for mental reasoning over physical sensation in order to help us feel better. This can depend on personality type too and you might identify with being a person who prefers one type of tool over the other. As well as using our bodies to ease or self soothe through stress, we can also use our logic to support us. Simply put, when we want to change how we feel, we can first change how we think.

First and foremost, stop. Pause the stream of thought that's constantly flowing through your mind. Distract away from mindlessness and notice what you were thinking about just now. Be aware of yourself as an entity which has conscious thought as part of its being. Step outside of conscious thought for a moment and become aware of it. Say it out loud, write it down, explore how it's making you feel. Are your thoughts helpful or unhelpful? Are they negative or positive? Are they repetitive or novel? Some people call this meta-cognition, which means thinking about thinking. If you need to, set up prompts so that you're sure to pause and think about your thoughts on a regular basis. Create a digital notification or a note on your fridge. Whenever you can, generate awareness of your thoughts so that they stop controlling you but rather become a servant to you gaining the life you desire.

Emotions are helpful signals trying to let us know that we need to attend to something important. We are evolutionarily wired to experience the range of emotions for adaptive reasons. A good example is a threat to our survival, which is a legitimate activator to the limbic system, amygdala and a host of stress hormones. However, there are times when our brains over-exert themselves in worry and stress when it's unnecessary. There are countless stressors in our twenty-first-century environments that do not require a fight, flight or freeze response. To name a few examples: your Wi-Fi stops working, there are too many emails in your inbox or a driver cuts you up on the road. There's really no need to burst into survival mode in any of these instances, however, the levels of stress we carry with us during these times is comparable to those we experience during a serious threat to our lives. In addition, neuroscience shows us that merely imagining a scenario can activate the same neurotransmitters as actually experiencing that same scenario. So having a realistic mindset really is the best way. One strategy at your disposal is to gain perspective. How important is this event, really? How much of your life is it going to impact? How long will this problem last? Is it worth getting upset about? On top of gaining a healthier perspective, try externalising your thinking by separating your true self (the permanent) from your thoughts or feelings (the transient) and realise what's a part of you and what's fleeting and external, which you can let go of, if you wish.

The neo-cortex brings with it the uniquely human trait of affective forecasting, that is, predicting what will happen in the future and how we'll feel about it. We base these forecasts on past events, experiences, emotions and outcomes. Our frontal lobes have organised and categorised our memories and learning in such a way that we don't even have to consciously think about a future event to guess how it will turn out. It's as though "we just know". But of course, we can't know, not really. The future is unwritten and there are so many routes it might take, most of which are currently incomprehensible to us because nature and science are constantly evolving, teaching us anew, every step of the way. We do not know what's around the next corner, or even whether the next corner will be there by the time we reach it. Or in fact, whether we'll reach it. You get my point … Affective forecasting essentially wastes a lot of energy when what we ought to be doing instead is focusing on the here and now, flourishing in our current moment. After all, the only real moment we ever have is this one, right here, right now. The past is already gone, the future isn't real yet. It never is, because it never arrives. Only this moment arrives. That's not to say we should never plan anything. An immense amount of joy comes from the excitement of an upcoming holiday or fun event. Bask in those emotions, for sure. Just leave the brain ache of affective forecasting if it's not bringing you joy.

What we call "negative emotions" aren't all bad. We probably don't need as many of them as we have in any given day and that's part of my personal mission, or purpose – to create positivity for people and organisations so that the world becomes a happier place. We do need to take more action in enhancing mental wellbeing for ourselves and each other. However, this is not about eradicating negative emotions because as I've said before, they have their very important place. So give them the limelight (for a short while), let them take centre stage (briefly). Allow yourself time to mope, get angry, be stressed, cry, punch a pillow, over think, over analyse, vent ... then leave it at that. Create boundaries for that stage show, discipline your negative emotions so they are heard and validated but not given the steering wheel. Your adaptive emotions remain in the driver's seat, just as long as you let the others have their say now and again. Placate the monster within. Ignoring it will only aggravate the beast! You're human, just like the rest of us. Everyone knows their monsters and any decent human being will accept you for taking the time to tame and train yours without the pretence that they don't exist. If you feel so inclined, talk your brain through the process. Tell it when you're offering it time to feel the nasties. Say "Okay brain, now's your time for anger, you've got 2 minutes, GO!" and then, "Thank you brain for alerting me to the fact that I'm upset, let's vent to a friend tomorrow, but now is the time to be calm." Your brain belongs to you and works well with boundaries and discipline, just like people do. You and your brain can be the very best of friends, so do your utmost to look after it and it will do its utmost to look after you in return.

Notice when you're catastrophising. This is when we think or feel disproportionately about an event, in that one negative occurrence will lead to another and another and without even trying, we arrive despairingly at the worst case scenario. Sheepishly, our hands go up when we admit we've all done this. We've all blown things out of proportion in the heat of an argument, or concerned ourselves with a hundred things we didn't need to think about, or taken the fast track route to the worst case scenario just because it all felt dismal at the time. That, and making comparative notions about mountains and molehills, is classic catastrophising. Some are self confessed fluent in it. More dramatic types might even like it a little bit, because it offers a rush. But it's unrealistic and pessimistic and elevates stress hormones that we don't need. American psychologist and author Susan Jeffers (2006) urges us to consider all the ways we've demonstrated resilience in our pasts in order to affirm how well we'll likely deal with difficulties going forwards. Take a breath, pause and stop that stream of thinking, gain your perspective and gently say to yourself, "I've got through hard times in the past and I'll get through this too." This is one truth we can all rightly say to ourselves, because our success rate for everything that life has thrown at us so far is 100%. How very empowering.

Remember, all thoughts are real to your brain, so whatever data you're inputting into that supercomputer inside your skull is the data it will use to determine the output of how to think, feel and behave. By thinking good thoughts, you train the neural pathways in that way and optimistic thinking becomes easier and easier over time, just like training in any other way. Repetition is key, creating habits is essential and the outcome is a more natural and authentic pattern of positivity in your life.

Two fun activities are to create your "best possible self" and the "best case scenario", both of which helpfully reframe negativity bias. When we recognise that we're being self critical or catastrophising, we can switch our thought processes to serve us more favourably. Rather than spiralling down the rabbit hole of "What's the worst that can happen?", focus on the best thing that could happen. Ask yourself, "What's the most amazing thing that could be next?" or "What will I do when I succeed?" and run with that. By doing this, you're constructing positive neural pathways and making way for desirable opportunities in your mind. Have you ever opened your mind to something different, perhaps following an inspiring conversation or during learning a new topic, only to find many more opportunities present themselves, as if by magic, in that very area of your life? It's not magic at all, it's simply that you've created space and flexibility for further potential and we have the capacity to do this even during tough times. You're not controlling external influences, but you are taking control of the things you pay attention to by taking the blinkers off and opening new doors. At the very least, by visualising your best possible self and exploring best case scenarios, you're boosting your happy hormones and may just be inviting fabulous things into your life in the process!

The quality of your thinking determines the quality of your life, because your thoughts are powerful and frequent. Training the brain just takes a little motivation and effort and whilst it's an organ rather than a muscle, getting it to learn how to behave works in the same way as building any other muscle in your body. Practise and repeat. And believe in it. If we think positively, then our brains become more adept at positive cognition and those types of emotions come more naturally to us. The more regularly a set of neurons fire together, the more readily they will fire together in the future. Increasing the experience of positivity within our neuronal network will train the brain to recognise positivity in our environment more readily, act more quickly on it and sit with it for longer periods of time. It's just like forming any other habit – the more we rehearse, the more adept our brains become. As it takes a mere 21 days to form a new habit and the average person has 29,711 days alive, it's worth a try.

Boost your happy hormones

Great news! Research has shown that desirable emotions activate the left prefrontal cortex (Breuning, 2015), so what can we do to help? We can purposely and regularly engage in strategies to boost happy hormones so that our baseline levels of contentment are higher.

Dopamine is the reward chemical and makes the quest towards meeting a need feel good and exciting. It motivates us to strive towards the important things in life. To increase your dopamine levels, move towards an unmet need and strive towards a goal that you haven't yet achieved. Rather than focus on the top of the mountain, set your sights on what's closer and more readily achievable. Set smaller goals, take smaller steps and you'll trigger more dopamine rewards for yourself.

Endorphins are triggered by pain and mask that pain with euphoria for short periods so that we can escape danger and protect our injuries. To get some of them, move around during long periods of stillness. If you're sitting at your work desk or on public transport, moving creates mini boosts of this hormone. Do some gentle exercise.

Oxytocin is the bonding hormone and is based on trust. It rewards us for finding social support and spending time with people we feel close to or safe with. Fire it up by finding your tribe! Locate the people you feel close with and those who make you feel safe. Surround yourself with people who make you feel good. Build trust with new people in small steps, by making progressive gestures to others when you want to create a lasting relationship with them. This will build your own oxytocin circuit and generate small releases of oxytocin from the reciprocal behaviours of others towards you. Or, simply cuddle your favourite person or pet, which will also do the trick!

Serotonin is related to personal strength and doing well, especially compared to others. So, remind yourself of all the areas in which you're great. Focus on your strengths, skills and achievements. Do more of what you're good at and accept compliments from others as genuine.

Of the 100 billion neurons we have to work with, it's decidedly beneficial to make as many of them as great as possible. We can change the way we see the world by changing our mindset. As Henry Ford, founder of the Ford Motor Company, put it, "whether you think you can or think you can't, you're right." So do what you can with this amazing resource and supercomputer you have at your disposal. Give some positivity techniques a go. One thing is for certain, your brain will be taking note!

EMOTIONAL INTELLIGENCE

Emotion = survival

First thing's first – emotions are all good. The definition of the word "emotional" is "relating to a person's emotions". Alternative definitions include, "arousing or characterised by intense feeling" and "having feelings that are easily excited and openly displayed". So there we have it. Being emotional is a good thing. It is societal judgements and accusations which have turned this wonderfully human (and indeed, arousing and exciting) attribute into something we have become afraid of, even ashamed of. Generally, being "emotional" somehow made its way into the category of personality traits we shy away from. Balderdash. (I've been waiting for an appropriate time to use that word!) Emotions are generated in the limbic system, one of the oldest parts of our brains, the absence of which would cause absolute havoc. In fact, we simply wouldn't survive. That's right, being emotional is necessary for our survival. We know that the role of the limbic system is to let you know when there's something wrong in your environment, something that you need to attend to fast, in order to preserve your life. You might say that survival of the fittest could in fact be survival of the most emotional.

We're all emotional

Interestingly, there are differences between the sexes when it comes to emotion recognition, regulation and expression. This may not come as a huge surprise, and of course there are always people at both ends of the spectrum and those who challenge the "average" data set. Researchers call these "outliers"; I call them interesting! But the data is there for us to ponder and the science is compelling. The amygdala is the brain's threat detector. The dorsomedial prefrontal cortex involves reasoning and emotion regulation. Brain imaging research shows that these two brain regions interact more in males, meaning that men have a more analytical approach when dealing with negativity, which can manifest in a cooler, calmer response to adversity as he considers his response whilst assessing the situation. Women, on the other hand, tend to have larger limbic systems, which enable them to experience emotions more acutely and be more readily able to identify, access and respond to different types of emotions. For any given situation, men will tend to exclude information they deem unnecessary, by way of simplifying their thought process to reach a solution. In that same situation, women will tend to bring in more empathy as they process what's going on. It's no wonder that miscommunications often occur when circumstances become emotionally charged. Neurologically, people are experiencing the exact same situation differently (Lungu et al., 2015).

Emotions are everywhere. In our family, friends, colleagues, language, books, song lyrics, films, social media, art, dance. We attribute emotions to colours, animals and even the weather! Our work can be emotive, mine certainly is. Did I embark on a career in supporting people's mental wellbeing because I'm supposedly higher on the hypothetical emotion scale or have I become more in tune with the wonderful interactions between thoughts, feelings and behaviours over time, through years of training and clinical experience? Your guess is as good as mine, but I suspect it's a bit of both, as with most things in life. One thing I know for sure, I was drawn to proactive wellbeing practices, because of how it makes me feel and the emotional impact it has.

When I first heard Bethany J. Adams (2020) talk about the role of emotional intelligence at work, I smiled as she uttered the words, "I'm successful in my work not in spite of my emotions, but because of them." How uplifting and reassuring for those of us who don't always have our emotions permanently in check (which is all of us, by the way). Also for those of us who sometimes experience a spill over of our personal lives into our work lives, because emotions don't stand behind the line waiting patiently until 5pm in order to come back and knock on the door (which again, is all of us … there's an obvious theme here). There's a little technique that I use which is to give my emotions permission to have their limelight. Offering our feelings time and space to have their say works in the same way as listening to another person have their say. It allows them to feel heard and dissipates the intensity. Calmness follows, because it can. So next time you feel those intense emotions rising, try saying to yourself, "Hello emotion, I see you're there and I'm going to give you some time a little later because what you've got to tell me is important, but for now let's focus on finishing this task and then I'm all ears for you!" Do a deal with your emotions and give yourself permission to ring fence some time just for them. All of them. They'll love you for it.

EQ for the win

It turns out that research into emotional intelligence (otherwise known as emotional quotient or EQ) demonstrates that it is just as important in day to day life as its better-known sibling, intelligence quotient (IQ), if not more so. The latter of the two is the one that we're a little more au fait with and there's an irony in that, which I hope will become apparent if it isn't already. A simple internet search of the difference between EQ and IQ generates descriptions defining EQ as an individual's ability to identify, evaluate and express emotions, whereas IQ is a score derived from one of several standardised tests designed to assess an individual's intelligence. Now, which sounds more compelling to you as a point of reference for living your best life?

If EQ is so vital to our ability to understand ourselves, interact well with one another and generally flourish, why do we know so little about it? It is a product of society, history, education, or a fixed mindset … take your pick! One reason is that our education system hasn't included this learning as a mandatory part of the curriculum. It has been deemed more important to work out whether Billy or Bunty will reach the finish line faster if Bunty is lighter in weight, is running with the wind (which is travelling at 14mph) and can sprint exponentially faster over a period of … talk about unnecessary brain ache! Don't get me wrong, mathematics is essential, of course. We use it every day and mustn't do away with it, nor other useful parts of the curriculum that we already offer to our younger generations. I'm simply saying that learning to feel, talk, express and support ourselves and others with emotional recognition, understanding and effective management is right up there in the important stakes too. Some schools are already taking great leaps towards incorporating these kinds of topics and they'll no doubt lead the way with their level-headed, well-rounded, empathic individuals! These things take time and I'm sure that one day EQ will be compulsory alongside the other brilliant sciences. Our future generations will certainly thank us for it.

Another reason we know so little about EQ is to do with our early experiences. When humans have babies, they don't simultaneously hear the thud of a great, shiny manual landing on their doorstep, complete with step by step instructions and detailed diagrams of how to teach these beings all there is to know about the multitude of feelings they're about to experience. In other words, there is no perfect guide to parenting. Adults having children haven't themselves been taught how to deal with this gargantuan spectrum of emotions, let alone have the wisdom and vocabulary to teach anyone else.

I'll let you into a secret: even us psychologists don't have it all figured out and we study the topic! I would certainly have appreciated and benefitted from some emotional coaching in school and even though I'm fortunate to have lived through a relatively calm childhood, I'm sure my parents would have benefitted from that hypothetical manual; they'd have read it from cover to cover, added their notes in the margins, tabbed some of the pages and thumbed through to the relevant sections in times of need – if only they'd heard that thud on their doorstep the day I arrived home with them. Bless you Mum and Dad for raising such an emotional human – for what it's worth, I think you did a great job. I also recognise that you're human too. It's quite the revelation, that moment we realise that our parents are just people like us, going through life the best way they can, having made all the same mistakes that we are making, with all the same dilemmas and decisions. It's a celebration and validation of what's just bloomin' well normal.

We really are all in this together, so why not make the journey a little easier and start learning about EQ right from the start. If you haven't realised yet, you're already doing it, if you've stayed with me up until this point and read the previous chapters. Well done to the emotional centres of your brain; those neurons in your prefrontal cortex and your limbic system have been firing wildly and making brand new connections. Nurture them, practise what you're learning, think of it often and you'll strengthen the wiring together of those neurons and synapses to carry this learning through your life. Do you see what we're doing here? We're making headway with our EQ as we go. Bravo brains.

Psychological safety

Forward thinking organisations carefully consider the concept of "psychological safety", which is being able to show one's true self and express emotions openly, without fear of negative consequences, such as a devolvement of self image or status. It is the safety of opening up and being vulnerable in the presence of others, by sharing thoughts and feelings. Organisations that are exploring this idea understand that they need to lead by example and create safe environments by encouraging active listening and an open and growth mindset. In 2012, Google embarked on Project Aristotle, an innovative study of hundreds of teams to investigate why some soared and others sank. Psychologists, sociologists, engineers and statisticians worked together for over a year, gathering data and formulating reasons for group and personal thriving in this vast company. Their conclusion was that the most important component of effective teams was psychological safety. In order to be highly effective, we don't just need smart goals and time management, we also need a hefty dollop of showing up as our authentic selves in the world, no matter what we've got going on or how we feel about it. Yay for emotions and yay for vulnerability!

Emotions and feelings

Confusingly, the terms "emotions" and "feelings" are often used interchangeably and that's because they're similar, of course. In fact, you'll read varying definitions in the research, which further implies that there's still so much we don't know about these complex topics. The science is building, which I find incredibly exciting! I shall attempt to make a useful distinction for those of you who are interested.

Emotions are automatic reactions, which are activated through neurotransmitters and hormones released by the brain following an emotionally charged event. Feelings are the conscious experiences of this automatic, neuro-physiological process. We tend to be more aware of our feelings and so these are what we most readily talk about. Many of us don't delve deeply enough to reach our actual emotions, so you could say that they're deeper or more specific. Emotions take more effort to articulate because they often sit subconsciously in the limbic system (the instinctual part of the brain where automatic responses to external stimuli are formed). Becoming more aware of emotions brings them into consciousness, where they are examined and analysed in the frontal lobe (the more developed, thinking part of the brain) and consequently, they are labelled as feelings. Clear as mud? Good! Let's explore a couple of examples. We declare a feeling of joy when we complete an exciting and important task. The motivation when approaching a goal is heightened by the release of a chemical called dopamine, which is one of the beautifully termed "happy hormones". This chemical is generated in the limbic system and is carried around our physiological system when we are approaching that reward, which keeps us striving towards it. This is the emotion. We feel envy when aware of desirable things others have which we don't. Serotonin is another one of the happy hormones and is associated with one-upmanship. It is depleted when someone is doing better than us. This is the emotion. Loretta Breuning founded the Inner Mammal Institute, with her fascinating perspective on these hormones and their evolutionary nature, bringing us back to the fact that we are, after all, animals by design.

One could argue that awareness of emotions is more important than awareness of feelings, because the health benefits are longer lasting when we feel good without consciously deciding to. Another reason to pop EQ high up on the agenda.

Recognising emotions

One of the blockers to living an emotionally aware and healthy life is that we don't learn how to recognise emotions in ourselves or others from a young age, nor do we realise the best strategies to express or manage them, even though these strategies help prevent problematic behaviours and consequences, reduce mental ill health and enhance relationships. We don't want to be around people who are brilliant at every physical endeavour there is to be brilliant at, or fill our teams with people who know all there is to know about processes and procedures. What we really want is to be surrounded by people in our personal and working lives who are flexible, inspiring and motivating. We want to be surrounded by people who are good at relationships, who can understand feelings and emotions and the impact of both. EQ enhances connection and deep love. EQ boosts productivity and success. EQ helps us make better decisions. I haven't found much wrong with it yet, to be honest.

I once had a manager who said to me, "Sometimes Vik, you have to just do what your manager tells you and get on with it, no matter how you feel about it." The rest of that meeting did not go well. Not because I became upset, which I may have done a few years earlier had such a situation arisen. With years of practising positivity under my belt, I somehow managed to harness the intensity of the subconscious (aka the emotion) flooding my limbic system and bring it into frontal lobe focus, in order to have a quick think about it. I remained calm and articulated my feelings and my emotions. I believe I did that well. What I didn't do so well was empathise with how my manager was doing in that moment and what brought her to say what she did. Fixed and negative mindsets tend to arise from something difficult or a fear that the person is trying to avoid. A little more time in frontal lobe focus and I could see that her comment wasn't about me. How useful it would have been for me to see that at the time. Perhaps I could have reconciled my manager's difficult emotions at the same time as my own.

How useful it would have been if we'd both been taught how to access and express our emotions effectively in provocative situations. I'm certain we could've ended that meeting in a more constructive way. Reflecting on this also makes me think about leadership. Bring to mind some of the people in your life right now who are in a leadership position, whether at work, at home or on a societal level. Maybe it's you that comes to mind; we are all leaders of sorts, even if the only person we're leading is our self. Transformational leaders understand their emotions and take the time to understand others. The outcomes are lowered attrition rates and less burnout, higher retention of motivated people in their teams. This is a huge part of the work I do with forward thinking organisations and I always learn from each and every one of them; at the very least it helps me to hone my own ability to empathise, accept and adapt. There's a whole area of positive leadership to explore, feel free to get in touch if you're interested!

Permission to feel

Back to EQ. Marc Brackett is the founding director of the Yale Centre for Emotional Intelligence and states the importance of recognising the cues your body offers, by pausing to check in and notice what physical sensations you're feeling and what they might mean. He says that understanding and labelling feelings and emotions in this way is a pre-requisite to expressing and regulating, which ultimately supports us in reducing harmful or distressing emotions and helps us feel better. None of this suggests that we ought not feel difficult emotions in the first place, in fact, Marc flies the flag for being right there with the feeling and accepting whatever it is. He simply wants us to stop allowing our feelings to take control over us. As he puts it, "give yourself and others permission to feel" (Brackett, 2020).

Indeed, it's easier to push emotions away, pretend they're not happening and suppress the thoughts we find too difficult to sit with. But this is maladaptive because emotions, like energy, don't simply disappear, they just move around and re-emerge somewhere else. This doesn't come naturally to most of us and now we know why, because we're not taught to deal with it from a young age, so by the time we become aware of what's happening, we've already formed a fair few unhelpful habits. We mustn't put pressure on ourselves to get it right all the time, but we can learn something new and begin putting wellness practices in place today. Even something as simple as stopping in the middle of a difficult emotion and asking yourself, "What's the story I'm telling myself right now?" and accepting whatever comes up. Then gently challenging the validity of it or exploring a different possibility, perhaps. Just like any habit, with time it becomes easier and eventually second nature. What better skill to develop than being able to recognise, understand, express and regulate your own emotional experiences? How many skills are more useful than emotional intelligence? Give it a go and remember to present yourself with your very own gold star certification in EQ when you make any kind of breakthrough! Every achievement is a milestone.

We can utilise those moments of heightened emotion to elicit our most amazing creations, because when we're in the flow of emotions, particularly difficult ones, our brains are at their most deeply receptive and reflective. We feel more. Or at least, we feel as though we feel more. These are the best times to express something outwardly in the form of a song lyric, a painting, a story. This is when we most authentically connect with people, because people can see right into our souls. We create bonds, inspire and energise others. It's a beneficial mechanism and a worthwhile reframe of something in our lives that we see as difficult to navigate. Some of the most successful artists, actors and singer songwriters talk of how they channel their emotional stories into their most renowned projects. I've heard people say they're not creative. I say they just haven't placed their emotions on the podium yet.

Your personality style somewhat determines how you make decisions and whether you lead with your heart or your head. Approximately half of the population check in with their logical brains immediately when a decision needs to be made. They allow their hearts to have a say too, of course, but ultimately it's the product of the pros and cons list and the conscious mental effort of thoroughly thinking things through that helps them decide. The other half of the population go straight to their hearts when there's a fork in the road and they need to choose which way to turn. They follow an instinct, based on how it feels over and above the weighting of the possible positives and negatives. We all have a heart and a head, thankfully. There are no tin men or lions amongst us. Ideally, we'll bring both characters into play if our impending decision is a life changing one. It's good to think, talk and consider the options and consequences. However, there's something to be said for trusting our instincts a little more and allowing our emotional minds to shine in these moments, because they're able to access parts of our worlds that we mightn't be aware of and that can be helpful.

Emotions are integral to our thinking, reasoning and decision making. Remember that contract with life we talked about earlier? It's the same deal with our emotions. We don't get the passion, excitement and enthusiasm without the anger, frustration and sadness. It's a package; all-inclusive and non-negotiable.

PART FOUR: ENABLING GREATNESS

MOVING THROUGH STUCKNESS

I'm not one to hover too long over a topic that causes anxiety for people, which stress does tend to do (poor stress, its only intention is to protect us!). Yet it's helpful to pause on the subject for a moment.

Get to know stress

Signs of stress vary from person to person and there are many manifestations, whether they be headaches, tummy upsets, hot flushes, lack of sleep, over eating, drinking, crying, over exercising, pretending ... and that's by no means an exhaustive list. Working out which ones are most prominent for you enables you to become more aware, so you're more likely to notice when they begin to arise. Early identification allows you to step back, take an examining look at the causes and consider your route out of the cycle. Stress isn't a random physiological response, it's telling us something significant is happening that we'd do well to be aware of. It might be imminent danger, or a task we need to complete in order to avoid negative consequences. It can be vital for our survival and is therefore conducive to our wellbeing. Yes, I'm saying that stress can be a good thing. It can be motivating, inspiring, movement-inducing, change making. It can also get too much. It can become chronically detrimental. It can impact our physical and mental health. This is what I call "stuckness". Stress is okay, to a point, until overwhelm takes hold and we are simply stuck with it for longer than we need to be. Either way, stress is always worth attending to and acting upon, as soon as we notice it.

Next time you begin to experience those symptoms of stress, stop and ask yourself what's going on and what it's telling you. Then tackle that before going about the rest of your day. Your body and mind will thank you for it.

More often than not, the underlying cause is quite simple. Most of the time, stress surfaces when you're not living in alignment with yourself. It's good news, because all you need to do is remind yourself, in any given situation, what your priority is. For me, I tend to return to, "the most important thing is to be authentic". Once you know what that priority is for you, then do it. The rest is (your perfectly formed) history.

Sometimes unexpected and sudden events occur in our lives and the shock and change that they bring induce stress, which is perfectly natural. It's our body's way of informing us that something is different and that we need to act in some way. It's our job to make sense of it with the wisest mind we can muster, which isn't easy amidst a tricky situation that came hurtling at us sideways. Take redundancy as an example. In my case, I was going about my work in a position I was proud to have, never dreamed of in fact, feeling safe in the knowledge that I had one of those "secure" jobs. Of course, there is no such thing and that's actually okay! The problem comes from having an expectation that things won't change or that we become complacent. I was due to have a meeting with my manager and we sat in an office with windows. Floor to ceiling windows looking out to everyone in the office. She entered the room with a pile of papers and a toilet roll, which I thought was a little odd. She asked how I was and I replied with that all time favourite British response, "I'm fine thank you, how are you?" She didn't answer my question. She read verbatim from the top of the pile of papers in her hands. I noticed her shaking and her voice trembling. It can't have been pleasant for her as she read my redundancy notice, which would take effect immediately. It wasn't pleasant for me either.

What happened was a fairly intense stress response. My amygdala reported the threat to my hypothalamus, producing cortisol to send through my adrenal glands and throughout the rest of my body. I froze, could hardly speak and had a flurry of difficult emotions. I felt shocked, hurt, afraid, angry. My heart rate increased, I began to shake and I'm not ashamed to admit that I cried. I was overwhelmed. The toilet roll made sense now as she handed it to me. She asked if I was okay. I said I would be, because somehow, deep down, there were also some other emotions emerging. I had a gut feeling that I'd be okay, even though I had no idea how in that moment. I had just come out of a serious relationship so wasn't feeling my strongest, I was selling my house and buying a new one, and now I was going to be without a job or steady income to pay the mortgage and bills which were all mine and mine alone. Yes, it was pretty stressful, I'd say!

Faint yet persistent positive emotions were still there, buried under the power of the stress response (that little almond shaped amygdala is so good at its job, a little too good at times!) but they were there. I brought them into focus as much as I could and over time this focus gave them strength and they became the prominent ones. I decided not to put myself through further stress of interviews to begin another one of those secure jobs. I made a decision to set up my own business. And so Positive Wellbeing was founded. The very day after my contract officially ended. A complete change in circumstances and a complete change in my working life. This decision was emotionally driven by my heart, I might add, because I had no idea how to go about being a businesswoman; I just knew I wanted to do it and I believed that I could.

As I write this, I'm still fairly new to being a business owner, so I'm learning and hopeful. Whatever happens, I know

I can get through it, adapt to all that life throws my way and create something shiny, new and exciting as a result. The ability to flex with the meandering rivers of life events is priceless. The stress was difficult, of course. It was a shock. It took me right out of my comfort zone, right out of my "safe" little bubble. It removed the security that I perceived I had, up to that point. Zander and Zander, a couple comprising of a family therapist and conductor of the Boston Philharmonic Orchestra, wrote a book about finding possibilities where there appear to be none (Zander & Zander, 2002). They suggest that we open our minds to new ways of thinking and most definitely step "outside the box" when we're faced with events that initially paralyze us.

Find the upside

Feeling unsafe and stress go hand in hand. It's not all plain sailing either. What is? My earnings now depend on the hard work I put in and is never guaranteed as with a salaried job, nor do I reap the rewards of all those faithful years in service. I don't get paid to go on holiday and if I'm poorly, I take time off without a financial buffer. However, I don't list these things with sorrow or longing. Quite the opposite. I feel freer than I've ever felt, with more opportunities, choices and autonomy than I ever thought possible. Most importantly, I have never felt so much meaning and purpose in my life as I do now, doing what I enjoy and carving my own path. My own path which is unlike anyone else's, because I'm doing what I enjoy and what I'm passionate about and I can decide what that is as my life moves through its inevitably changeable seasons. And hey, I had time to write a book, because I scheduled time in my own diary for it. If only in that moment, when my manager read my redundancy notice to me, I could've stopped stress in its tracks and told it that this would actually be one of the best things that could've happened. If you reflect on stressful life events of your own, you'll likely find one or two that caused you to make the most amazing changes in your lives, those which took you in a direction you never dreamed of. Australian speaker and author Christine Caine says that when we feel like we're being buried, we're actually being planted.

Safety is paramount, of course. But take a moment to explore where you get your security from. To answer "money" is easy, but is that true? I used to think it helped, and it does, to a point. But since I was put in the position of needing to think more about this, I realise that I get safety and security from much deeper places. To me, safety is: letting all my emotions show and those close to me standing by me, being accepted, loved and cared for even on my worst days and during my darkest times, openness and honesty, knowing enough to understand and make sense of my situation, feeling well and healthy with available medical support, access to snacks and a place to nip to the loo! I'm actually serious, money doesn't feature here. Kindness features. Connection features. Health features. Above all else, authenticity features.

Wellbeing economy

Widening our scope here, there's a societal movement called the wellbeing economy, which puts people and the planet first. Traditionally, we've come to accept that profit is the most important indicator of success, which is why most economies use gross domestic product (GDP) as the deciding factor of how they spend their budgets. Some countries (including New Zealand and Iceland) are replacing GDP with wellbeing, allowing money to be spent on things that are most important to citizens, including things that make people feel good. No matter who you are, whatever roles you play, you're just as influential in being a part of this shift towards a better culture, one that values human life above cashflow. It seems so obvious, yet we have work to do to achieve a culture that prioritises happiness. We need to change the narrative, have the conversations, say what we think and play our part in creating the world we all deserve. People and the planet.

Happiness. What else matters, really?

Immediate response

By now, we all know that stressful events can occur in the blink of an eye, without warning, or they can occur cumulatively when we weren't quite paying enough attention to our own self care regime. When something comes at us sideways, blindsides us or pulls the rug from underneath us, there are little things that help.

First, pause. Give yourself the most precious gift of a little time. Just a few seconds if that's all you have. It might be all you need to put the brakes on the initial stress response of retaliation or anger.

Know yourself and stand by yourself. Treat yourself as you would treat a best friend and be there for yourself in all the ways you need to be.

Get practical. Work out what the facts are and try to put the emotion to one side, just for a moment, in order to see the situation objectively. See the bigger picture and zoom out on a larger portion of your life to examine how much and for how long this will have an impact.

Bring in compassion, for yourself and for others. There are a whole host of reasons that events occur and reasons why people do things they do. At times it can feel terribly intentional and unfair, but for the most part, people are simply whizzing around their own worlds trying their best and making mistakes along the way. Inevitably, some of their mistakes will affect you, and vice versa. Live as you want to live, act in accordance with your values and don't let the actions of others change the way you would naturally tend to behave.

Finally, make small steps to move forwards through the stress and hurt. Focus on the present rather than the past or the future, especially the advantages in any given situation or on any given day. You can only control your own behaviours and whatever else is going on out there is going to happen because of a million different reasons. Finding peace with this and accepting all as it is, will be the foundation of successfully moving through a difficult time, back to happiness.

Playfulness over hurtness

Ideally, we'd replace as much stress as we can with playfulness. Where possible, lose your self consciousness, lose track of time and spend time without purpose; just be and have a good time while you're at it. Put everything else aside for just that moment and be playful. Wouldn't it be wonderful to live with unbridled energy and unlimited enthusiasm for novel things, just as children do? How splendid to see the world with such imagination and creativity once more, the way we all once did. We don't have to lose out on playfulness just because we're adults. All we need to do is find our own ways to play.

I'm not suggesting you relieve your stress by getting out the plastic teacups and hosting a make believe tea party (but do go ahead, if it makes you smile!), I'm suggesting you get up early to the wonder of a sunrise, taking a blanket and a hot flask to a high hill. Run to the top and collapse when you get there. Look up and smile when you get caught in a rain shower, or dance if your self consciousness allows. Sing to yourself in the mirror, pretend you're the protagonist of your favourite movie, splash around in the sea or jump in for the sake of a big splash! The possibilities of playfulness as an adult are endless. All I know is I've never heard of anyone who looked back over their life and wished they were more serious.

The affliction that many of us suffer from without even realising it, is that we live our adult years from a place of hurt, because of the mental and emotional accumulation of everything that's ever happened to us. I don't believe there's a diagnosis for this, so let's call it "hurtness". Right now, if you were faced with an important decision, you'd weigh up the pros and cons, or you'd follow your gut instinct, but either way, whether it be your head or your heart that decides, your choice will be coloured by past pains, rejections and judgements that you'd prefer to avoid happening again. If we meet our life decisions with this knowledge, knowing that lens we're choosing our path through, we can learn to live from a place of love instead of hurt. To do this, we must let our hearts have a say. But not only must we hear our broken hearts, we must hear our vibrant, beating, enthusiastic, playful, carefree, wondrous, curious hearts too, because that's where the magic lies. That is the essence of life. No matter what we've been through, we can always choose to step out, go for it, live. In actual fact, you don't need to change anything about yourself in this way, you just need to tap back into who you are and truly be yourself. I'm giving you permission, in fact, I'm pleading with you to do just that.

PERSPECTIVE

What was your biggest problem, three problems ago? When this question was first posed, it really made me stop and think. I couldn't remember. What a light bulb moment! Instant realisation that our problems take over our lives, consume us completely, yet three problems later, we can't even recollect what was so catastrophically wrong back then. This might seem like a pessimistic viewpoint but it's actually the opposite; once we realise that the most difficult, stressful, awkward moments in our lives are in fact transient, even forgettable, it blasts them into a different level of significance – perhaps insignificance.

The mantra to remind ourselves on a daily basis is, "In three problems time, I won't bring this problem to mind". We put far too much weight, spend far too much time and expend far too much energy on problems as they arise, when most of them do in fact sort themselves out, somehow. You may have heard the ancient proverb, "It'll be alright in the end, and if it's not alright, it's not the end", which is somewhat calming. A bit like the notion I mentioned earlier, that your success rate for surviving everything that life has thrown at you so far is 100%. That's pretty good going. It also makes you a very strong and resilient person, actually.

Perspective is key then. Accepting that, just as we have seasons in our world (because we're turning on an axis at approximately 1,000 miles per hour), we have seasons in our lives too (perhaps because we're spinning so fast … it certainly feels like it at times too!). Some days are glorious, warm, calm, with a gentle breeze that will cause no harm. Some days are brutal, harsh, with storms that cause destruction and devastation. Sometimes seasons are predictable, sometimes they're not. Life is like that. We fair better when we're prepared, stocked with tools that we can protect ourselves with and be more resilient when bad weather arrives. After all, there's always some calm after the storm. Always. We just have to make it to the other side.

When it comes to emotions, humans have an inherent inability to imagine much other than their current state of being or feeling. Take common physiological states, for example. When we're hungry, it's difficult to bring to mind the feeling of satiation or engorgement. When we're cold, imagining being warm doesn't come easily. Deeper emotional states are the same. We feel sad around people because of something they have which is a perceived lack in our own lives. Recognising that these feelings are transient and knowing that they have a shelf life means we can accept the feelings as important messengers, informing us of something meaningful that we value. Yet, it is temporary and will all work itself out – in the end. You see, this is how problems work. They consume us, they overwhelm us, they create a feeling of being stuck. They're just today's problems and that's really all they'll ever be.

Make greener grass

Dial down the problem focused thinking and turn up the gratitude. Worrying about the problem won't resolve it or make it any lighter. The opposite, in fact. We can train our brains into a different way of thinking. Rather than a lack, what is the gain in the current situation? Acknowledge the good, seek the benefits and bask in those. Be selfish, in the most life-affirming, joyous and exciting way. What was the problem again? It seems smaller now. The point isn't to talk yourself out of having the problem, because we need to address issues that require our attention. My point is, can we celebrate any part of it? There's a bright side to every story, every circumstance, and nobody should make us feel we can't be glad about that, least of all ourselves. The grass is green enough, exactly where we are.

Believe that wonderful things are about to happen. Know that everything is going to be okay. Enjoy it, it's happening (whatever "it" is for you). Often, when we hear those words uttered by someone who cares about us, we feel calmer. How many times have you thought back to your younger self and thought, "I wish I hadn't worried so much". The reason? Because in the end, it really was all okay. Sometimes only just, but it was okay in the end. It makes me consider this thing we call intuition. I'm not intending to become ethereal here, I'm actually talking about something intrinsic to animals. A fantastically useful tool that we all possess. We don't pay enough attention to it because we can't see it, touch it, and because of its intangible nature, even the best scientists struggle to test it. That doesn't mean it's worthless or unreal. On the contrary, if we tune in to our intuition more, we learn about ourselves, make better decisions that make us happier and of course, we become authentic.

Trust your instinct

Intuition is made up of logic and abstraction and has four components: instinct, experience, faith and reason. Our instinct is the root of our survival, by giving us physiological signals when danger is looming or things don't seem right, so that we behave in ways that quite literally save our lives. Without instinct, we would probably be extinct by now. Our experience is a bank of events that have occurred in our lives, with associated judgements, feelings and memories. Some would argue that experience is more tangible than instinct, because it "actually" happened. But as we only see the world through our own lens (and we know that our lens can be tinted), others would argue that experience is relatively subjective. Then there's faith, which is complete trust or confidence in someone or something. Finally, reason, which is the power of the mind to think, understand and form judgements based on what is actually possible.

These four components of intuition lie in the two broad categories of the head and the heart, which are alternative words for logic and abstraction. Together, these create what we experience as wholeheartedness, which is absolute commitment to sincerity.

Neurological studies show us that the intuitive part of our brain knows the right answer long before the more analytical, conscious part. What's happening is that patterns from our past experience and our environment are being processed by the brain, in order to make a rapid, in the moment decision. It's when we start to over think something that our judgement can become clouded. We begin to analyse and reason, when our gut feeling had all the information it needed all along, to enable us to reach the right decision.

Remember, to live your best life, the aim is not to become perfect but to become authentic. This comes with sincerity and commitment, aka wholeheartedness. So, all we need to do is tune in to our intuition, hear it, trust it and follow it. There's no manual for this, perhaps because it's such a unique and individual endeavour for each of us. That doesn't mean it's difficult to achieve. In fact, it's quite simple really.

Honing intuition

Here are the best ways to hone your intuition and let it work most effectively for you.

Listen. Take notice of any moment you believe your intuition is at play. Schedule in some silence.

Feel. You might have a physiological response to a person

or situation, such as increased heart rate, goosebumps or a shiver. This is your body instinctually telling you something, based on all the information it has to date. Brain–body connections are real, such as feeling "sick to our stomach" when something goes wrong.

Keep good company. Surround yourself with people who make you feel good, who you trust, those who show you the best version of yourself. They are the ones who will give you the space to listen to your intuition and guide you along the route to what you really want.

Be mindful. Intuition requires as much information as possible in order to make the best decisions for you in any given moment. Noticing and taking in as much as we can about our surroundings is the best fuel we can offer to our instinctual potential. So slow down, look around, remove distractions and let the world in.

What if something goes wrong? When our radar breaks, when something didn't work out the way we'd hoped or when we lose our grip on reality, we often turn to external sources for advice (friends, family, social media, the internet). Whilst it's useful to gather other perspectives and different opinions, it can steer us away from our own path and that means we don't behave so authentically. Therefore, if we're unsure of what to do about any given situation or problem, we need to sit with the uncertainty for long enough, so that our intuition can surge back into action. Clarity often comes from uncertainty, if we accept the latter for long enough. Why would we choose to be sure but miserable when we can instead be unsure but wholehearted? Ask yourself, "What would I do if I had no fear?"

Ask future you

A technique that I like to use and recommend time and time again for others, is to project yourself into the future and look back on yourself in this moment. What would your older, wiser self say to your current self? The way I frame this is, "How would future Vik help present Vik?" Is there anything you'd suggest, recommend or regret? Listen to yourself, then act accordingly. Our greatest life goal ought to be to look back over our time on Earth and say, "Everything I ever did was just right, at that time". If we check in with our conscience and our hearts and they both feel good about something, then it's the right decision. So do what you need and what you enjoy and leave the rest. It's true that we can only rise up from being down, so the lows are necessary in order to experience the highs. Everything teaches us something. Another helpful mantra is, "Where's the good?" Sometimes it's obvious, sometimes we have to dig for it and sometimes it takes a while to surface, but training our minds to locate the positives and focus on them acts as a booster to our overall health.

Dopamine is a neurochemical that assists in counteracting the potentially harmful effects of the stress hormone cortisol and is involved in driving us towards a reward. It's linked to approach motivation and allows us to feel great in the process of seeking and finding what we desire, whether it be food, a relationship or a great bargain! Society, however, has us focusing too heavily on the end result, so we miss out on the wonderful benefits of this "happy hormone" in the run up to the reward. Have you ever noticed yourself thinking, "once I get a pay rise, I can do more of what I enjoy", or "when I find my dream home, I'll be happy"? It's commonplace to look forward towards end goals, but it's somewhat an illusion too, because once we reach that goal, we don't become infinitely satisfied. Instead, we immediately seek out the next reward and focus on the end goal of that. Rarely do we enjoy the process or the smaller sparks along the way.

When asked, many people would project themselves forwards to a time when they believe their lives would be better, such as when they've finished decorating their home, or are sitting on a sunny beach abroad, or married to their partner, or have their own family. The problem with this is that we're effectively wishing our lives away, constantly. We work for the weekends. We live for the big moments. Going back to my technique of projecting yourself forwards that I described above, imagine a candid discussion with yourself on your deathbed (bear with me!) and ask yourself whether you're glad you ran with blinkered vision towards every big life event or whether you could have spent more time basking in the wild and windy paths you took to get there, noticing all the joys along the way. If you were given the last decade of your life to re-live, would it be worth doing that a little more? Future you (that's the one looking back at you now, a decade into the future) is begging you to start now. Enjoy the dopamine. Enjoy the ride. The road is just as good as the end. The summit is nothing without the majestic mountain leading up to it.

IT'S ABOUT TIME

Time management remains a popular topic for training in work settings. Often, this abstract concept that we call "time" is our reason for not getting things done, for not completing tasks or finishing our to-do list. It's also the reason we don't look after ourselves or others properly. We simply seem to run out of time. Poor time, getting the blame for everything we ought to do, but don't. If only time weren't so fixed ... hold on a moment (if I may take some of this time we speak of, to consider this). What if there's a different way to perceive time?

Time for your personality

Personality profiling gives us useful insights into how different people view and experience the world in different ways. Not only is it extremely useful to get to know ourselves more intimately, but it is fascinating to see the profound impact that understanding others has on our interactions. By adapting our style, language and behaviour, we learn to get the most out of our relationships and create space for everyone to thrive in situations that may otherwise elicit only one-sided contentment or even conflict.

The first personality profiling tool I became certified to use was based on the well known Myers-Briggs Type Inventory. One of the four personality type preferences is about how we like to manage our time. Actually, it goes deeper than that, right down to how we inherently view time, how we experience time and the ways that our relationship with time manifests in our behaviours.

At one end of the preference scale, we have people who see time as fixed and precious. They don't waste other people's time and do not appreciate people wasting theirs. Every task is anticipated to take a certain amount of time and pressure ensues when this allotted time begins to run out, as if there will be no more. Lists are a favourite method of tracking progress and checking items off the to-do list brings great satisfaction. In fact, if a list is fully checked off at the end of the day (or another set amount of time allocated to said to-do list) that makes for a very buoyant mood. These people tend to use time based language more and ticking clocks get additional mentions. Superb planners, these people are organised and like to get tasks underway as soon as they are aware of what needs to be done, so that they can finish the work as soon as possible. Focus on work can become so intense that breaks are forgotten and play must wait until after work. There are clear boundaries between time in the office and time at home, almost as though a switch is flicked and one or the other is temporarily turned off. These are people who, from a young age (perhaps at school or college) would complete assignments early so as not to feel the heavy burden of stress by leaving things until the last minute. In fact, last minute deadlines cause alarm, to the point of anxiety in some cases, and that ticking clock almost sounds louder as the deadlines loom. People at this end of the preference scale are, in MBTI terms, "Judgers". As an aside, it has nothing to do with judging or being judgemental.

Let's fly right across to the other end of this preference scale, where those who experience time much more loosely and fluidly sit. There is less emphasis placed upon time in order to get things done, in fact, there is a general sense that more time can always be found, or somehow created. Spontaneity abounds as anything can crop up at any moment, without feeling like too much of a strain on the current task at hand. It will all get done eventually and that causes no alarm. Upon receiving a task, people may or may not begin right away, they will continue in bursts as and when the mood takes them, interspersed right alongside all other aspects of life, including fun. Work and play live side by side and do not appear to disturb one another if they're in the same space. These are the people who completed their school or college assignments right at the last minute, perhaps in the early hours of the day of the deadline, without anxiety. In fact, stress plays an important role in achieving their best work as if it somehow intensifies creativity and effort. As though the looming deadline is the very thing that gets people's juices flowing and generates action. In MBTI terms, people at this end of the preference scale are called "Perceivers". Again, this has nothing to do with how perceptive they are.

Our relationship with time

Have you ever thought about how often we make reference to this abstract concept that is time? The way we talk about saving time, as though we can gather it up and pop it in a trinket box for later. Then there's spare time, which somehow suggests that there are bubbles of time floating around that we can catch and add to the time we already have, because it's going spare.

What about all the things that time can do? Time flies, time heals all wounds, time costs money and time will tell. Time is with us, always. And it's powerful if we believe all those magical things it's capable of. So it's best that we make a great relationship with it then, I'd say. Make time your friend, see it as an asset and live peacefully alongside whatever time you have for whatever it is that you need to do.

Research shows that satisfaction with how we spend our time is one of the biggest predictors of wellbeing (Bormans,

2011). We must take time for ourselves every day, in whatever way that is meaningful to us. We feel better when we've achieved something, no matter how small, or how much or little time that achievement has taken. We need to take complete responsibility for our own time and stop blaming poor time for not being there for us, or for not being enough. Time is there and it is enough, we just need to change our relationship with it; we need to alter our mindset. Blaming external factors means that nothing changes. Your time reflects your choices and in turn, reflects your whole life. So be content with how you're spending it! We have absolutely no control over the passing of time, it is what it is. We can neither stop it, nor go back in time, we can't speed it up or slow it down, no matter how much we wish we could. The question is, what do you have control over and what are you going to do about it? The time is now.

Time really is precious

Shocking and sad life events, such as the loss of a loved one or news of a terminal illness, act as a catalyst for reflecting on the time we have on Earth and how we want to spend it.

Dad had been visiting his doctor for a few years, which was a big deal for a generally fit and healthy man. Each time, he left with a slightly different spin on the generic advice to watch and wait, see how it feels in a few weeks. Nobody seemed to know why his discomfort was occurring, nor did they offer further investigation. Not until his symptoms became severe enough for us to intervene as a family and make strong requests for a scan, which was eventually granted. Following the consultation, Dad called with the results and I'll never forget that sentence, "Hiya duck, it's malignant." A lump fills my throat even thinking about it. I remember standing still in the middle of the road, the phone pressed against my ear and everything seeming suddenly silent. It was as though the whole world stopped, leaving a huge void and nothing else. I remember thinking, "No, this can't be happening, I can't handle this." What I felt was utter desperation. What I said was, "Okay, we're going to do whatever we need to get through this." Dad is an optimist, always finding a way and taking life in his stride with a reasonable attitude to things. I wanted to reflect that back at him when he might have needed it and so we both opted for normality. Within minutes, we were talking about making a cup of tea, as though the mention of something inane would take the dreadful news away. It didn't, of course, but it did put us on the track to moving through this and getting on with things anyway.

That day was a nothing day. I was in a daze, where everything seemed pointless and nothing else mattered, at all. Nothing except us, as a family, not letting this news or diagnosis get the better of us. The following morning, I had a nano second of peace before I remembered what had happened the day before and the world around me seemed to cease to exist once more. It was hard to get up and get going that day. But the determination of helping Mum and Dad through this was what kept me going. We were all being, on the outside at least, incredibly resilient.

The coming year was stressful for us. Dad became incredibly poorly and had to be helped with simple, daily tasks. A man who had been the director of a successful company and built half our house with his bare hands, could hardly eat or drink. So confused about the TV remote that he needed help to use it. Commenting on the moving patterns on the hospital walls even though they were blank. All because of that nasty tumour and the cocktail of drugs he had to take. It was the saddest thing to witness. As if that weren't enough, seeing Mum work tirelessly through each day and night to do everything she could to keep him as well as he could be, turning her hand to the household chores that would normally be his. I'm biased, but these were good people going through the worst time. Grossly unfair. I'm sure that nobody would wish this on anyone, ever.

Countless visits to the consultant and prayers from us all that the medication was doing its job in halting progression of the illness and reducing the mass. Then on one visit, Dad was informed that the tumour was growing again and they offered to operate right away. Without hesitation, they both took the offer, even though it came with the unthinkable risk. It was a significant and complicated procedure. But they were in good hands, the surgeon was excellent and they wanted the chance of living life as normal once again. Tremendous courage and a vision towards a better life.

That was another phone call I'll never forget; this time it was Mum's voice, trying to sound calm and strong, "We're not going home tonight. They're going to keep Dad in and operate in the morning." She was doing everything in her power to not tell me that this could be the last time I saw my father, but when she suggested I join them that night, for a few days in the room next to the hospital that she'd book for us, I knew that's what she was thinking. She was putting all her might into gathering up the fragments and do what was needed for all of us, even though she too was in the midst of the crisis. This is a strength of hers that I admire. Our world had stopped once more and she was navigating through it as best she could.

I don't remember much at all about the hours in between that phone call and arriving at the hospital that night, but I do remember the next morning as we got up, met Dad on the ward and walked with him as he was taken on the trolley down the warren of corridors. At the final set of doors, we were asked not to go any further and I think my heart stopped for a short time. I watched Dad disappear behind the doors and into theatre as he raised his thumb to let us know he'd be okay. This was something we did when we knew the other was worried for us. It made me cry and smile at the same time. The truth was that none of us knew if he'd be okay. We were told there were no guarantees. I'd done my best to tell Dad that he was and always would be my inspiration. Just in case. There was no way that I wasn't letting him know what a positive influence he'd been in my life.

I don't think any of us remember much about the hours we waited, it seemed like a lifetime. Was the clock on the wall standing still or going backwards?! Then came the call from the ward and I locked my eyes onto Mum's face to gauge any micro movement as she received the news. I've never been so relieved in all my days. Dad was alright and the operation had gone well. We could see him. Turning on our heels, we did all but run through the hospital and to his bedside, where he was groggy but awake. My mum and sister listened intently as the surgeon updated them and I sat at Dad's side, holding his hand, repeating the best snippets of what I could hear – anything that sounded like good news. He nodded and said, "That's good, duck" and it seemed like finally, everything was going to be okay. We could begin life once more and focus on recovery. That really was all that mattered. Time began to move again, slowly, but surely. We weren't granted an easy road ahead and there were still bumps to overcome, but we had been given the most precious gift of all – time.

Spend it wisely

When my dad had his operation, I was midway through the final year of my clinical psychology doctorate, which is the busiest year of training, lectures, work placement days and a hefty thesis. I'd have given it all up in a heartbeat. When Dad's 60th birthday came around, we didn't know whether he'd celebrate another. So it was a no brainer to miss that week of teaching, which ironically, was all about chronic health issues. At that point, I'd have accepted being removed from training if it had come to it. That thing I'd spent years working towards and studying for, the dream of becoming Dr Barnes. None of it mattered in the great scheme of things. Nothing matters as much as life and love. That was the biggest lesson I've ever learned in perspective. It showed me that time, the way we spend it and who we spend it with, is the most important thing.

So, be ruthless with your time. That means deciding what matters most to you and spending more time on that, whether it be hobbies, tasks or people. Fill your time as much as you can with whatever gives you most purpose, meaning and happiness. Often, we spend too much time on things that give us no or little reward when there's no real need to do so. Learn to say no to those drains on your time, where there is no need to say yes. Turn off notifications if you don't need them and choose when to let them in. Only allow yourself to be interrupted when you're okay to be. Other people respect our time only as much as we respect it ourselves. If you're seen as someone who values their own time, as someone who chooses to spend their time on things most precious, others will realise this and will value your time too. Happy people tend to slow down their pace and use time effectively, yet simply. Productivity and satisfaction do not have to mean filling every minute, even if it's with fun. Haste and hurry aren't what nature intended. A purposeful life is a life of purpose.

THAT'S ONE SMALL STEP

On rocky ground

Earlier, I mentioned a time (we'll no longer think of the word "time" in the same way) in my working life that was difficult – the redundancy. Part of what I found so hard was the shock. That, on top of the desire for things not to change. It was only when I began to accept and adapt to things being different, by taking the next small steps, that my mental health began to flourish again.

A few years before the redundancy, I'd been given the fantastic opportunity to fully direct my attention towards my passion of positive psychology and immerse myself into creating and leading a wellbeing programme for a large UK based organisation. I became a "high flyer" by my humble standards, travelled a lot, had my hotel and meal expenses paid and was known as the national expert in my field.

Six months before, I'd experienced the highlight of my working life up to that point – offering mental health aid to Hurricane Irma survivors in the British Virgin Islands. Spending time with one of the most famous and well known people in the world. Fully engaged in leading the most worthwhile project I could imagine – setting up mental health support for people who previously hadn't access to any. I was on top of the world in many ways. It was surreal and not a trip that I thought "someone like me" would ever have the chance to take.

Then came the monthly meeting with my manager who promptly read my unexpected redundancy letter, with immediate effect. I had no clue what to do. I was, quite simply, in shock.

Almost simultaneously, the realisation of what else was happening in my life dawned. It was like a heavy curtain dropping around me. That relationship I was in, the person I was set to spend my life with, was ending. Right at the same time. It was emotional turmoil and I knew I wouldn't have his support when I told him about the redundancy. I was right. I wasn't alone, not at all, but I felt it.

I was also moving house. What was meant to be an exciting and joyous occasion was stressful and unmotivating.

All of this was about change. Change that I didn't see coming and certainly didn't choose. I tried hard to keep as many things as I could the same, as if it would help me stay grounded. I needed familiarity but it was ebbing away and nothing I could do was stopping the floor breaking away beneath me. I felt like I was losing control of all these important aspects of my life and that's a very uncomfortable feeling.

Moreover, I had no idea what the next day looked like, or the next month or year, let alone the rest of my life. All I could think was that it looked like I had to start again, in so many ways. My home, relationship and work all got thrust into the air and fragments were landing all around me, with no way of me being able to put these broken pieces back together again. I wouldn't wish it on anyone.

Stepping towards the horizon

This is where the wonderful art of positivity comes in. Eventually (and we now know that we must allow ourselves to go through the heavy emotions before we reach the lighter ones) I began picking up those fragments, some old and some new, and pieced together a fresh version of my life. Better, in fact. I had been given the gift of being able to start again, start afresh, with a clean slate. I never would have chosen that, not in a million lifetimes, because it felt terribly unsafe at the time. But it forced me to make changes that were good for me and I am happier, not in spite of it, but because of it.

I was brutally thrust out of my comfort zone and my life took a 180 degree turn. It removed a lot of security I perceived that I had. But I can honestly say that, even though the promise of security was reduced, the sense of purpose, meaning and moments of joy have been so much greater since then. Home, relationships and work became more about me, as in, they reflect who I am now, rather than who I had somehow thought I needed to be. I had been set free to create the life I wanted. A bit like moving into a new home, painting all the walls white and adding whatever colour, furniture and decoration you like. It was an odd realisation that only by going through all that turmoil and upset, was I able to invent a life that I chose. What a rare opportunity! All those aspects of enjoyment, acceptance and authenticity that we've been exploring, came together in the superb way that they do, most noticeably following periods of instability.

Whilst backpacking in New Zealand, I remember being rather taken by a quote plastered along the side of a bus, which read: "what a caterpillar calls the end, the rest of the world calls a butterfly." I instantly loved this sentiment, which I took to mean two things. First, the all important art of perspective comes into play. From the standpoint of the caterpillar, life is over, at least as he knows it. How fascinating to think that, as far as we're aware, these little furry creatures have no idea that they're only in their embryonic stage of being, that their destiny is to become a butterfly. From the perspective of an outsider, something truly magical happens and becoming a butterfly isn't a bad way to end up. Second, the struggle that a caterpillar goes through in order to reach its full potential as butterfly is astonishing. The humble caterpillar has to fall apart and decompose until there is nothing left of it. From a decomposed mess, the butterfly forms, slowly, from scratch. If that isn't a metaphor for bouncing back resiliently after a setback, then I don't know what is. It can certainly feel as though the cards that life deals to us take their toll and leave us in a big old mess, devoid of any sign of life as we knew it.

Repairing and rebuilding ourselves takes time, energy and effort and can seem like too high a mountain to climb. Then, tiny step by tiny step, things change, situations improve, bodies mend, hearts heal and minds strengthen. If we were to take another's perspective, we might see ourselves as more beautiful following the breaking down of ourselves. Much like the Japanese see more beauty in possessions that, once broken, they mend with gold. They believe these hold even more beauty than the perfectly formed and unbroken original. They even have a word for it and that word is *kintsukuroi*. How wonderful to see the world that way, if we were to not only see possessions as such, but humans too. You may have had your share of knocks over your lifetime, but that makes you more inspiring, interesting and awesome! Not to mention, ironically, more "normal" (as in, living in the majority alongside the rest of us mere mortals who are definitely not perfect).

When we're facing a huge change and we can't imagine ever making it through to the other side, I use the analogy of hiking up a huge hill. One with boulders, streams, pits and bogs. From the bottom, we may peer at the seemingly unreachable summit and wonder how we'll ever make it there with all these barriers in our way. There's no clear path and each direction has something ready to halt progress. Approaching life in this way isn't effective. Rather than trying to make it straight to the top, we need to focus instead on the next small step; what's right in front of us and how we navigate that. Hop atop that boulder, because the vista changes from up there. Examine the stream, there might be a stepping stone to springboard across to the other side. We mustn't stand for too long staring at the summit with our hands on our hips and a furrowed brow, feeling agitated, because we may be on boggy ground and that's what gets us stuck.

Moving is progress, even if it's backwards. Sometimes a step back can be the best way to see the world in a different way and try something different. By contemplating and achieving one step at a time, before we know it we've made headway around corners, up and down dales and are closer to the summit without even realising it. By moving steadily and constantly, we avoid becoming stuck. Not only does that shift our mindset to one of constant mastery, it also puts us into a state of moment to moment mindfulness and enables us to enjoy the ride, not just the destination. There's something empowering about only having to worry about the part of the path that's right ahead of you, relieving the pressure of all things that may lurk around the corners. No matter how big the problem before you seems. Continuing to take those small steps also stops us becoming stuck; after all, we know what happens if we stand in a bog for too long.

Growth after crisis

Just a few months after I began writing my book, something huge happened, to all of us. Humans connected, locally, nationally and globally, over an unexpected, unique and shared experience. The global pandemic of COVID-19. It fascinated me from the outset. I was less worried, more intrigued. I wasn't so fearful as I was hopeful. For all the things I had in my life that I was grateful for, for all the changes we'd make as a society, for the better, for the greater good. We'd been advised into lockdown (which I found to be a harsh word, generating all sorts of anxieties for people; when my Texan friend told me that the Fort Worth mayor, Betsy Price, was advising, "Y'all stay home", somehow it seemed friendlier).

It seemed to happen so fast, which made it suddenly get serious. From hearing about the rise in cases on the news, to being instructed by the government to stay indoors and only leave the house under very few, restricted circumstances. It was extreme, unusual and of course bizarre. Yet alongside the pressure was release, alongside the craze was calm. It was comforting that we were all in the same boat, to have this collective understanding, to know that everyone was hoping for the same outcome. I had these moments of realisation that I had no "fear of missing out", because I knew that nobody else in the world was doing anything more exciting than me. I had a newfound respect and love for staying at home, because it was the only place to be; the best place to be. I "saw" more people every day than before, granted, on video calling platforms, but still. We saw each other more authentically. We began checking in with one another without any real need to, other than to be kind and stay connected. Work meetings became less formal. Conversations about mental health became more acceptable. I felt more at ease in some ways, when the city quietened down, when cars were hardly heard and crowds disappeared.

I missed hobbies, festivals and travel yet hoped for a positive impact on the environment. Looking up at a clear, blue sky, free of planes or contrails. Dazzling sunsets through clear skies of little smog. Bright stars seen with reduced light pollution. Noticing how peaceful it was at night, or the array of wildlife sounds heard without the hum of traffic noise. Animals adapted quickly to humans giving them space on earth, taking to the parks, gardens and even streets in the middle of town because we were less of a threat. On the first three evenings of lockdown I saw a fox outside my house, which I'd only seen once before, the entire time I'd lived there.

The world had been interrupted, yet at the same time, nature had stopped being interrupted. Re-addressing the environmental balance, perhaps. I've always been a fan of Sir David Attenborough and his voyages around the world, exposing us to all manner of weird and wonderful creatures that we'd know little about otherwise. The patron of Population Matters, a campaign to influence policy makers, communities and individuals to make necessary changes for sustainability. With a vision of decent living standards for all, humans and animals alike, on a healthy, biodiverse planet. Not least, by promoting ways in which we can learn matters of the greater good. Virtually impossible to solve, he says, with ever more people going about their lives blindly having a detrimental effect on the world. In the time it took me to type this very paragraph (2 minutes and 5 seconds to be exact), the population rose by 347 people. I know this because there's a world population count on their website. Astounding. If every one of those people does something to help, however small, it will make a significant difference.

The pandemic was affecting everything and we were jolted into interacting with our world differently. In these ways, what a magnificent experience. Possibly an event that will happen once in our lifetime, perhaps never in the next generations. Putting a positive spin on it, I remember going for my allotted daily, lone walk as I chatted on the phone to my parents (who I could no longer visit) as we marvelled at how magnificent it was to stop and think about the experience. An experience that you couldn't create if you tried, couldn't imagine if you hadn't been there. An experience to behold.

Simultaneously, I had a good dollop of guilt for trying to find the good. After all, people were dying. I cared about that, my thoughts went out to them and their loved ones. In addition, I didn't stay upbeat the whole time. Lockdown became tiring and very, very dull. Social activities were thwarted, events cancelled and I missed my loved ones and my hobbies. People began to get more frustrated over time and businesses suffered. I had times where I lost motivation and couldn't see the point in anything. I also felt more intense loneliness than I'd ever imagined. I worried more and more about the death toll, people I cared about and people I didn't even know, because of the devastation this disease was causing. The whole time, I felt it was teaching us something. I had a feeling that society might change for the better. I wondered about how it would feel when we're out the other side and we can properly reflect on the whole process. This may just change the world for good and whilst it has come with terrible impact, it may also be what we need to jolt ourselves into a different mindset. Are we realising what's important in life now? Are we more grateful for interactions with our friends and family? Do we all spend more time outdoors enjoying the benefits of nature, whatever the weather?

So how was it possible to have such nice emotions alongside such devastating news? I thought about that question a lot and wondered whether it was akin to the idea of the contract we have with life, that we get the good and the bad and that's the deal. Or perhaps it was akin to enjoying being the "up person" as well as being raw and real and down at times too. I was realising that human emotions are much more complex than even I, a psychologist who has studied and worked in this field for two decades, had understood before. I forgave myself for feeling like this global upheaval might have a silver lining. That forgiveness came because the some of the best outcomes were for the greater good. Society could re-prioritise some of its goals. The government could re-address some of its policies. Communities could come together and support one another. People could realise the value of goods and services. Waste could reduce. Respect could be enhanced for our leaders and the law. Flora and fauna could flourish. Wildlife could emerge. Pollution could fall. Carbon footprints could diminish. The Earth's resources could begin to replenish.

Sometimes we need to take a step back and look at what's happening around us, then decide what to do next or at least, how to be amidst it (hint: acceptance). Perhaps this was the Earth's way of giving us all a good telling off for not looking after it properly. Something about that concept made me take a deep breath and smile. We had been told to be by ourselves and think about what we've done! Another nod towards the wellbeing economy and a happier existence overall.

Perhaps all the world needs is love.

HOW TO BE HAPPY

One of the most common questions I'm asked in my work is, "How can we be happier?" and my response obviously differs depending on whether I'm working with an individual or an organisation and what the circumstances and needs are. I offer bespoke wellbeing consultation to forward thinking organisations that want to put mental wellbeing and happiness of people at the forefront of their agenda. Because it's the right thing to do.

We are people first and only after that should we identify ourselves by our roles. Go ahead and introduce yourself to me now, tell me about yourself. I bet you started with your name, occupation and where you're from. Perhaps then something about your role within the family or extracurricular activity. But this is not the essence of who we are. These are merely labels which describe some of the roles that we undertake. First and foremost we are humans, with senses and emotions and experiences and memories and ... so much more than roles and job titles. How to be happy often begins with the realisation of this and the exploration of who you really are, or who you want to be for the rest of your life. I delve into people's personality types, bring their strengths to the surface, hone their values, find ways they can get into that wondrous state of flow, explore their passions and what they want to be able to say about their one wonderful life when they look back upon it. I'd like to look back and say, "For the most part, I was happy. For always, I was authentic."

Part of the work I do is about helping people find ways to boost their own happy hormones! It sounds weird I know, but it's true. We've learned how neurotransmitters carry chemicals around the brain and which hormones make us feel good and boost our wellbeing. We also know that engaging in particular activities and strategies creates this chemical movement. I don't cause happiness for people, I simply get them to a place where they understand themselves and what they can do in order to generate their own feel good chemicals. I facilitate the process of people and organisations creating opportunities to be their best. It's a wonderful job.

When we tune into what truly makes us tick, we learn new ways to replicate as much of that in our daily lives as possible, exponentially growing our sense of meaning, purpose and overall wellness. If we're enjoying our work and home lives, we do more for our organisations and communities. If our organisations and governments value our wellbeing, we're more productive and successful. It's a two way street.

True happiness has several components. It's about how we see ourselves, engaging in self care, increasing self confidence, being true to ourselves and finding true meaning in what we do. It's about our relationships, kindness, connection, sharing honest feelings and being heard, being loved and belonging, having access to support and reciprocating for others. It's about engaging with all we have around us, nature, awe, gratitude, training our fabulous brains towards positivity bias. It's about being every last bit of our fantastic selves and being authentically human.

Hopefully you've had some realisations or new learnings that you can take into your future and feel good about. Just one thing will do. That's all it takes to catalyse movement and be the best version of yourself. There are lots of similar resources online, for example, the Greater Good Science

Center, which is a great platform for even more practical ideas relating to some of the topics we've discussed.

There are so many ways we can feel happier and they'll be different for each one of you. My wish is that you find your own way to shine and feel amazing while you're at it.

Happiness is free. And it's there for the taking. It's waiting patiently for you to open the door so that it can be a part of your life. It's up to you to let it run wild; to free happiness.

WHO AM I TO TELL YOU THIS?

I've spent a long time learning, researching and practising clinical and positive psychology, but I've also lived through a lot of difficulty and all the emotions that go with it. I definitely don't have all the answers and you don't have to agree with everything I believe. That's part of the beauty of how we're all the same but different. I wanted to share my thoughts in the hope that it celebrates you and all that you are. In the end, I'm just somebody who hopes it will make a positive difference and somebody who believes that it can. What does all of this mean to you? That's entirely up to you to decide. Take away whatever chapter, verse or message that resonates with you and make whatever small changes in your life that you believe will work. Be wildly and wonderfully you, in whatever ways feel right. Find happiness where you can, when you can. We're here once, so that's really all we need to do.

I gave you a sneaky peek of my darkest times, some of which weren't so long ago, as I began writing. I admitted to you, my fellow positive deviants, that I didn't think I'd live through it, or know whether I wanted to. I felt like some of the most important parts of my life had taken a 180 degree turn without my desire or intention, when I wasn't looking, to a point of great turmoil. I found everything really, really hard.

Yet, when I was recently asked the question, "Do mostly good or bad things happen to you?" I answered heartily "Oh, good things!" without hesitation. And when asked, "Do you see yourself as a fortunate person?" I responded definitely "Yes", without doubt.

My questioner must have noticed my eyes widen as I surprised myself, hearing my own voice and those cheery responses. Given the events that had unfolded around me in the months before, the fact that I wasn't where I wanted to be at the wonderful young age of 38 in any way whatsoever, how on earth was I still so adamant that I was in such a good position? It had to be something about the way I'd been living my life the past 10 years and all those positive habits I'd created in the orbit of my own little world.

To me, the interesting thing is where I am now, following such a dismal outlook. Somehow, I'm happy, even happier than before in fact and I actually did live through it. I didn't just survive, I thrived. Not because I'm superhuman, or because I knew exactly what to do, but because of something deep within me that kept chipping away. Call it hope, call it optimism, call it perseverance or relentless stubbornness! Whatever it is, I truly believe it was borne out of a mixture of an inherent desire to be happy, plus years of practising ways to be just that. Not forgetting, of course, the stupendously brilliant people in my life who supported me through those times. To all of this and all of them, I owe my life and am eternally grateful.

THE ENDING

Actually, it's still just the beginning. The time is now for you to go about your days (and thus, your lives) with good intention. Become a positive deviant.

Thank you for giving me your time. As you now know, time is your most precious commodity so I hope it's been worth it and I hope you see your time on this earth differently as a result. Thank you also for being open minded and reading the lot, I am very grateful and in awe of you for that.

Have you been reflecting on each chapter one by one, making notes and changes in your life as you read along? By now, you've at least begun to paint a colourful picture of how to live your best lives – it all has to do with being wholehearted and authentic.

We're supporting the whole spectrum of mental health by enhancing opportunities for wellbeing. Remember, we all have a part to play, not only in our own lives but in the lives of others and the world at large. We have the power to make a positive impact. My question to you is: Are you with me on this?

It's not rocket science. It's simply about being humanly happy.

WANT MORE?

I'm always learning new ways to embed positive psychology into everything that I do. I share new hints and tips on social media in the hope of inspiring others to do the same. I'd love to connect with you – find me on social media such as Instagram, Twitter and LinkedIn @DrVikkiBarnes or take a look at my website (www.drvikkibarnes.com) if you'd like a consultation or bespoke programme for you or your organisation.

I wish you happiness, wherever you may find it.

SUGGESTIONS FOR ACTION

Health is mental

Notice where you and others are on the mental health spectrum

Talk about mental health and be open to expressing it

Desire to be happy

The most important choice you'll ever make is whether or not to be happy

Mental wellbeing is free and enjoyable

Kindness and gratitude

Bring to mind one thing you're grateful to have right now

Keep a gratitude journal

Write down three good things before bed

Engage in one random act of kindness every day

Connection

Boost your oxytocin by spending time with people who make you feel good

Live in alignment with your natural personality style

Do good for the environment; give back to a world that supports you

Spend time alone to connect with yourself

A quiet mind

Simply notice, whatever is currently around you right now

Find a time and place that enables regular, mindful practice

Release the pressure and expectation

Non-judgementally name things

Breathe

Flow

Find hobbies that challenge you just beyond your current skill level

Fully immerse yourself and remove distractions

Awe in nature

Get outdoors and let nature nurture

Focus on your senses; what you can see, hear, smell, touch and taste

Step away from screens and turn off notifications

Go for an awe walk

Enjoyment

Re-learn and return to play

Allow your negative and repetitive thoughts to pass by

Enjoy whatever you have; be the envied one

Acceptance

Let go of the need to control everything

Know that you're always mostly okay

Refuse to blame

Vulnerability

Seek support when you need it, from a colleague, friend or professional

Vulnerability is emotional freedom and honesty

Talk openly about vulnerability

Remember, vulnerability is a great strength

Courage

Stay true to yourself

Say "yes" to the things that matter to you

Know when to remain neutral and when to intervene in another person's struggle

Put yourself out there for a loved one's sake

Failure

Remember that nothing in our universe is meant to be perfect

Avoid the "black and white" thinking trap

Beware of righteousness

Celebrating the "negatives"

Let regret teach you what matters

Share your shame stories with someone you trust

Allow yourself to feel every emotion you have the capacity to feel

Authenticity

The aim isn't to become perfect, but to become authentic

Express yourself. Worry less what others think. Have a good time

Be honest from the outset; it's a form of kindness

Your contract with life includes the good and the bad

Nurture your soft front

Check in with your heart as well as your head

Whatever you do, do it wholeheartedly

Certainties

Accept that uncertainty is okay

Be in control of you, that's it

See death as a teacher and live your life while you have it

Know that whatever your current situation, it will change

Happy brain, happy body

Ask yourself each day, "how am I feeling?" and "what do I need?"

Create your stress toolkit

Decipher whether you need a physical or mental tool

Keep your brain well by boosting your happy hormones

Emotional intelligence

Give all your emotions air time

Create a safe environment for free expression without repercussion

Be an emotional leader

Give yourself permission to feel

Moving through stuckness

Get to know your own stress, recognise and express it

Pause

Be self compassionate

See the bigger picture and take small steps

Perspective

Reflect on past problems to gain perspective on new ones

Hone your intuition

Ask your future self what your present self needs

It's about time

Understand your personal relationship with time

Know that others view time differently

Be ruthless and spend your time wisely

See time as the biggest gift

That's one small step

Shift focus from the end goal to the next small milestone

Take a small step and the rest will follow

Focus on the resources you have

Stay motivated by noting the positives

How to be happy

Explore who you are, aside from your roles and responsibilities

Spend time with people and things that make you feel good

Re-visit the chapters in this book, find what resonates, then do that

Most importantly, enjoy it. It's happening!

REFERENCES AND RESOURCES

Adams, B. J. (2020, March 26). *Bring Your Emotions To Work!* [Video]. TEDxVillanovaU. https://www.youtube.com/watch?v=4S4wzNX0oOA

Bormans, L. (2011). *The World Book of Happiness.* Firefly Books.

Brackett, M. (2020). *Permission to Feel.* Celadon Books.

Breuning, L. G. (2015). *Habits of a Happy Brain: Retrain Your Brain to Boost Your Serotonin, Dopamine, Oxytocin, & Endorphin Levels* (1st ed.). Adams Media.

Brown, B. (2010). *The Gifts of Imperfection: Let Go of Who You Think You're Supposed to Be and Embrace Who You Are* (1st ed.). Hazelden Publishing.

David, S. (2016). *Emotional Agility: Get Unstuck, Embrace Change, and Thrive in Work and Life* (1st ed.). Avery.

Dietrich, A. (2004). Neurocognitive mechanisms underlying the experience of flow. *Consciousness and Cognition, 13*(4), 746–761. https://doi.org/10.1016/j.concog.2004.07.002

Elk, M., Arciniegas Gomez, M. A., Zwaag, W., Schie, H. T., & Sauter, D. (2019). The neural correlates of the awe experience: Reduced default mode network activity during feelings of awe. *Human Brain Mapping*, https://pubmed.ncbi.nlm.nih.gov/31062899. https://doi.org/10.1002/hbm.24616

Gilbert, E. (2016). *Big Magic: Creative Living Beyond Fear* (Reprint ed.). Riverhead Books.

Good Life Project. (2021). *Good Life Project Podcast*. https://www.goodlifeproject.com/podcast

Greater Good Science Center. (2021). *Happiness*. https://greatergood.berkeley.edu/topic/happiness

Gruber, M. J., Gelman, B. D., & Ranganath, C. (2014). States of curiosity modulate hippocampus-dependent learning via the dopaminergic circuit. *Neuron, 84*(2), 486–496. https://doi.org/10.1016/j.neuron.2014.08.060

Halifax, J. (2011, September 2). *Compassion and the True Meaning of Empathy* [Video]. TED Talks. https://www.ted.com/talks/joan_halifax_compassion_and_the_true_meaning_of_empathy

Hanson, R. (2020, June 18). *The Science of Positive Brain Change*. https://www.rickhanson.net/the-science-of-positive-brain-change

Inner Mammal Institute. (2020, January 1). *Inner Mammal Institute*. https://innermammalinstitute.org

Jeffers, S. (2006). *Feel the Fear . . . and Do It Anyway* (20th Anniversary ed.). Ballantine Books.

Knost, L. R. (2013). *Two Thousand Kisses a Day: Gentle Parenting Through the Ages and Stages (A Little Hearts Handbook)*. Little Hearts Books, LLC.

Lungu, O., Potvin, S., Tikàsz, A., & Mendrek, A. (2015). Sex differences in effective fronto-limbic connectivity during negative emotion processing. *Psychoneuroendocrinology, 62*, 180–188. https://doi.org/10.1016/j.psyneuen.2015.08.012

MacLean, P. D. (1990). *The Triune Brain in Evolution: Role in Paleocerebral Functions* (1990th ed.). Springer.

Nature Editorial. (2018). A new way to capture the brain's electrical symphony. *Nature*. https://www.nature.com/articles/d41586-018-06694-6?error=cookies_not_supported&code=df0db5b1-f652-461b-8231-80e58586a7c1

Otting, G. L. (2020). *Limitless: How to Ignore Everybody, Carve Your Own Path, and Live Your Best Life* (Reprint ed.). Ideapress Publishing.

Perel, E. (2020). Therapist, author and speaker. https://www.estherperel.com

re:Work. (n.d.). https://rework.withgoogle.com/print/guides/5721312655835136

Seppala, E. (2017, June 28). *Connectedness & Health: The Science of Social Connection*. The Center for Compassion and Altruism Research and Education. http://ccare.stanford.edu/uncategorized/connectedness-health-the-science-of-social-connection-infographic

Singer, M. A. (2007). *The Untethered Soul: The Journey Beyond Yourself* (1st ed.). New Harbinger Publications/Noetic Books.

Sturm, V. E., Datta, S., Roy, A. R. K., Sible, I. J., Kosik, E. L., Veziris, C. R., Chow, T. E., Morris, N. A., Neuhaus, J., Kramer, J. H., Miller, B. L., Holley, S. R., & Keltner, D. (2020). Big smile, small self: Awe walks promote prosocial positive emotions in older adults. *Emotion*, https://psycnet.apa.org/record/2020-69974-001. https://doi.org/10.1037/emo0000876

The Myers & Briggs Foundation – MBTI® Basics. (2021). 2003–2021, The Myers and Briggs Foundation. https://www.myersbriggs.org/my-mbti-personality-type/mbti-basics

Tolle, E. (2008). *A New Earth: Awakening to Your Life's Purpose* (Reprint ed.). Penguin.

Valikhani, A., Rahmati Kankat, L., Hariri, P., Salehi, S., & Moustafa, A. A. (2019). Examining the mediating role of stress in the relationship between mindfulness and depression and anxiety: testing the mindfulness stress-buffering model. *Journal of Rational-Emotive & Cognitive-Behavior Therapy, 38*(1), 14–25. https://doi.org/10.1007/s10942-019-00321-7

Wellbeing Economy Alliance. (2020, December 17). *Home*. https://wellbeingeconomy.org

White, M. P., Alcock, I., Grellier, J., Wheeler, B. W., Hartig, T., Warber, S. L., Bone, A., Depledge, M. H., & Fleming, L. E. (2019). Spending at least 120 minutes a week in nature is associated with good health and wellbeing. *Scientific Reports, 9*(1), https://www.sciencedaily.com/releases/2019/06/190613095227.htm. https://doi.org/10.1038/s41598-019-44097-3

Zander, R. S., & Zander, B. (2002). *The Art of Possibility: Transforming Professional and Personal Life* (Rev ed.). Penguin Books.

Zhivotovskaya, E. (2020). *20 body and mind tools to overcome anxiety*. The Flourishing Centre. https://theflourishingcenter.com/20tools

ACKNOWLEDGEMENTS

Mum & Dad. Not because it's expected that an author's first book should be dedicated to her parents, but because I am grateful for the roots they planted upon which I grew, and the wings they nurtured with which I flew. Thanks for all you give, wholeheartedly and authentically. I couldn't have done any of this without you.

Vik's Book Team! Writing the book was one thing but getting it ready for publishing was another and I'm so grateful I wasn't alone in this. Thank you for your kindness and time, which all helped me keep going right through to the end. Brilliant beta readers: Clive Betts, Eric Moeller and June Handford. Super proofreader and much needed sounding board: Caroline Watson. Creative cover designer: Emma Chu. Fabulous formatter: Al Wadlan (also for the cover image). You are all my book stars and I couldn't have completed it without your support.

Those who generously gave their time to cheerlead and promote me along the way and empowered me to believe I could do it. Pam Cox, Robert Harrison, Stanny Post, Nikki Antonio-Gadsdon, Sir Richard Branson, Dr Pat Gwyer, Romy Meuter, Charlie Ioannou, Abigail Pierce, Arti Manani, Tracey Duke, Greg Bateman, Simon Scott-Nelson, Carolyn Jarecki,

Rob Baker, Carola Becker, Judy Salmon, George Anderson, Emma Skedd-Baker, Michael Tingsager, Ben Morton, Calvin Niles, Dan Love, Chris Bentley, Simon J Marton, David Green and of course, Cumbar.

The people at the international positive psychology conference in Utrecht 2019, who were the first to hear about my book as the idea popped into my mind. Your enthusiasm motivated me to start.

The man on my positive psychology masterclass in Bristol who told me that I'd broken the mould as a clinical psychologist. Comments like that mean a lot and leave a lasting impression.

And last but definitely not least, my wonderfully supportive family and friends who believe in every crazy idea I ever have and come along for the ride with every fanciful dream I ever follow. Thank you for being a part of my life that will always bring me smiles.

Sir Richard Branson's words on the cover were kindly given following my work on Necker Island and the British Virgin Islands.

Every effort has been made to properly reference and acknowledge all who have given advice and testimonials.

@DrVikkiBarnes

www.drvikkibarnes.com

Printed in Great Britain
by Amazon